HERBS

JUDITH HANN

DELICIOUS RECIPES
AND GROWING TIPS TO
TRANSFORM YOUR FOOD

HERBS

NOURISH
EAT WELL, LIVE WELL

HERBS
Judith Hann

First published in the UK and USA in 2017 by
Nourish, an imprint of Watkins Media Limited
19 Cecil Court
London WC2N 4EZ

enquiries@nourishbooks.com

Managing Editors: Rebecca Woods and Kate Fox
Editor: Wendy Hobson
Designer: Georgina Hewitt
Production: Uzma Taj
Commissioned photography: Tamin Jones
Food Stylist: Rebecca Woods
Prop Stylist: Jennifer Kay

A CIP record for this book is available from the
British Library

ISBN: 978-1-84899-282-5

10 9 8 7 6 5 4 3 2

Typeset in Arno Pro
Colour reproduction by XY Digital
Printed in China

Publisher's note
While every care has been taken in compiling the recipes
for this book, Watkins Media Limited, or any other
persons who have been involved in working on this
publication, cannot accept responsibility for any errors
or omissions, inadvertent or not, that may be found in
the recipes or text, nor for any problems that may arise
as a result of preparing one of these recipes. If you are
pregnant or breastfeeding or have any special dietary
requirements or medical conditions, it is advisable to
consult a medical professional before following any of
the recipes contained in this book.

NOTES ON THE RECIPES
Unless otherwise stated:
Use medium eggs, fruit and vegetables
Use fresh ingredients, including vegetables, herbs
 and chillies.
Wash fresh herbs and pat dry before use
Do not mix metric and imperial measurements
 1 tsp = 5ml 1 tbsp = 15ml 1 cup = 240ml
Oven temperatures are for a conventional oven;
 adjust times and temperatures for fan ovens
 according to the manufacturer's instructions

nourishbooks.com

CONTENTS

FOREWORD
MY LIFE WITH HERBS

Herbs have taken over my life. They have been catalysts in the kitchen, liberating my cooking by encouraging me to be more creative. And they have also helped me to become a serious plants woman, using the different shades of green, the texture and shape of the leaves, their intoxicating aroma and their glorious flowers to transform the look of my garden. When I harvest these beautiful herbs every day, they soon transform the look and the taste of my food too.

I first realized their benefits when I used a small range of herbs, grown in pots at my London home. But when we decided to move to the country, I looked for the perfect opportunity to grow herbs on a larger scale. We found a small farm in the Cotswolds with decaying buildings surrounded by neglected, jungly land. But near the farmhouse was a sheltered walled area, with poor, free-draining soil, once used to raise pigs – perfect for cultivating Mediterranean herbs like rosemary, thyme and oregano. An added bonus was that there were shaded corners where the soil could be improved for more demanding herbs.

Cultivating this derelict pig yard, then growing, harvesting and cooking every culinary herb I could track down, has provided me with plants that have elevated my cooking to a new level. It has been exciting and inspiring.

I drew the plan (pictured opposite) for my herb garden over 20 years ago, before any herbs were planted. It followed months spent reading every book on herbs I could find in a London library, as well as visiting many famous gardens. At one point my impatient husband said: "It is time to stop reading and start digging." And I've never looked back.

The tumbledown pig yard had the remains of Cotswold stone walls. After they had been rebuilt, they provided shelter for the herb plants, trapped their wonderful scents and also provided wall space for figs, grapes, roses and morello cherries. We made a small central pond to house frogs to eat the slugs which eat the herbs. There was enough ground around this pond to have four formal beds, with an area to one side for annual salad leaves and a pudding bed where I could grow sweet cicely, angelica, lavender and other herbs used in desserts.

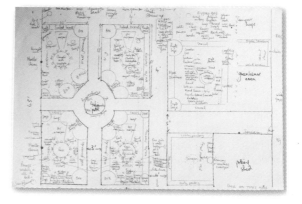

Now I am surprised and delighted by how my enthusiasm is inspiring other people and to find that herbs are improving their lives, too. In particular, I get so much pleasure when children become interested. I gave a selection of herb plants to two local village primary schools, for children to use in cookery lessons and to attract bees and butterflies. And my two young granddaughters have been helping me plant annual seeds since they were aged two and four. Because of feeling so involved, they enjoy collecting different herbs, leaves and flowers and making beautiful mixed salads with them, which they tuck into with the rest of the family.

Our younger son, who had leukaemia as a teenager, persuaded me to start herb courses, to raise money for research into the disease. I teach people from gardening clubs, herb groups and garden training courses, as well as enthusiasts who just want to spend a day learning how to grow and cook good food. The response has been fantastic. People now travel from other parts of the world to join a course, some rip out their garden plants and replace them with dozens of herbs, others write enthusiastic magazine articles or blogs about my garden, or send me rare herb plants through the post. I have even had herb recipes named after me, including a cupcake made with sweet cicely! It has become obvious that herbs inspire passionate interest.

All this is hard work and means summer holidays are impossible. But during a winter break in Thailand, the hotel chef approached me and said: "Please help us. I know you are a herb expert." He had recognized me from TV, Googled me and discovered my herb courses (Hann's Herbs). It became a working holiday, teaching the staff the best herbs to grow in the hotel's new garden. So herbs have not only taken over my life, they are taking over my world.

COOKING WITH HERBS

Nothing transforms food as much as herbs. They bring depths of flavour to other ingredients. As we move away from rich, salty recipes, they are used increasingly to enhance the taste of food. And as well as tasting wonderful, they smell and look enticing and bring colour and texture to the plate. So when you use these gods of the kitchen, you cook with all your senses.

Supermarket sales of herbs are increasing, but the range available is small, they are expensive and, even when chemicals are used to prolong shelf life, they soon go stale and yellow. By growing your own herbs, in pots or in the garden, you can make any recipe without worrying what's in stock in your local shop. You can pick your herbs just before cooking, using precisely the amount you need, knowing this freshness brings the optimum flavour.

The frustration cooks can feel when they can't buy the herbs they need for a recipe was shown when a man I had never seen in my life turned up unannounced on my doorstep one morning, emerging from a car full of children and suitcases. He was on the way to Cornwall and had ordered some lobsters to be delivered to him there for a special recipe that needed chervil. But he could not find it anywhere. Finally, a local greengrocer, who knew my passion for herbs, pointed him in my direction. To reward his persistent enthusiasm I gave him a huge bag of chervil as a holiday present, just as I give away cut herbs and plants to friends, neighbours and to chefs when we eat out locally in pubs and restaurants where they really care about good food.

Many of my favourite herbs are hard to find in shops, but are easy to grow in the garden. Herbs like chervil, lovage,

sorrel and oregano are rarely stocked, but they thrive year after year in my herb garden and are used in dozens of my best recipes, like Guinea Fowl with Lovage and Lime (see page 52) or Sorrel Ice Cream (see page 111).

The memorable flavour of herbs like these has helped to change the culinary code that insisted certain herbs always went with particular ingredients – for example, rosemary or mint with lamb and parsley with fish. Now people experiment. As my recipes show, I use rosemary with orchard fruits, like pears, and lamb with lavender. Mint is as likely to be used in desserts as meat dishes and parsley at its best is made into pesto or fresh sauces.

Herbs build up layers of flavour, with "hard" herbs like bay, thyme and rosemary used for long cooking, infusing a dish with their characteristic, earthy tastes. "Soft" herbs like basil, coriander/cilantro, parsley or chervil are added at the end of cooking, almost like a seasoning. They can be scattered over a dish, mixed into a sauce, or added to lightly dressed salad leaves. Many of them, like chervil, have elegant leaves which look perfect as a decoration. When I am chopping these soft herbs, I do it at the last minute so the juices do not dry up and the herbs do not lose their impact on our taste buds. I use a very sharp knife to avoid bruising, so the juices are retained inside the herb leaves, achieving taste, aroma and beauty all on one plate.

When we sit down to a meal, my guests sometimes find a vase of freshly picked herbs in the middle of the table, which they often nibble and always talk about. I explain how other parts of the world have been more loyal to herbs – something we in the West are just waking up to.

I tell them about the custom in the Middle East of having a bowl of herbs served with mezze, which is still done today. Women believe eating them makes them healthy and remember the old tradition that these herbs keep their men away from rivals.

Sorrel and chervil have always been sold on French market stalls and the same can be said of oregano and basil in Italy and coriander/cilantro in Asia. It seems clear to me that when it comes to herbs, the rest of the world has a lot of catching up to do.

GROWING HERBS

Herbs are far easier to grow than other plants, demanding very little, but giving so much. Anyone can do it, on a small scale in pots on the windowsill or on a larger scale outside, whether you grow them in a mixed flowerbed or allotment, or whether you have the luxury of a separate herb garden at home. And more and more people want this connection with the earth by growing herbs, so they can have the great pleasure and inspiration in their cooking that I have been so lucky to experience.

The world's largest gardening charity, The Royal Horticultural Society, found in a survey that the majority of 16 to 24-year-olds grow plants. "They are now more interested in showing off their herb gardens or tomato plants than they are in clubbing," it said. Renting homes is becoming common for a lot of people. Growing herbs and vegetables can be more of a challenge if you have no garden and cannot find an allotment. But herbs grow well in pots and window boxes, while indoor green walls are also being set up, where herbs can be grown in vertical planters.

Matthew Pottage who, at 29, became the youngest curator at the RHS in 2015, says people in the survey find that growing herbs is a creative way to spend time away from a computer or phone screen. "We've realized that a handful of fresh coriander/cilantro or basil, which you can serve with a tomato and mozzarella salad, is so simple and good after a stressful day at work," he said.

Herbs take up much less time and space than vegetables, making them the perfect convenience food. They can be harvested throughout the year, just before you want them for a recipe. You eat them when you need them, not when the crop's maturity dictates. Herbs can also be left to their own devices and rarely need watering because so many thrive in hot, dry conditions. They are also economical. A small bunch of herbs makes a huge impact on a dish.

Their aroma and sheer beauty mean that herbs can also help to reduce stress. A group of different herbs will reward you with varying shades of green in your flowerbed or window box, many unusual leaf shapes and glorious flowers in a rainbow of colours. These attract bees and butterflies and ward off unwanted insects, too. Growing them provides the opportunity to crush the scented leaves between your fingers for the joy of the smell of rosemary, bay or mint.

The scent released as I work in the herb garden brings back memories. Sweet cicely makes me think of the aniseed-tasting liquorice I used to buy at a sweet shop after school. Moroccan mint reminds me of a wonderful holiday in Marrakech and the Atlas Mountains, or the spearmint I chewed as a child. And thyme takes me back to scented walks among the wild plants of Provence.

CHOOSING YOUR HERBS

Before you can work out a plan for planting, you need to look at the space you have available – whether in a garden or in containers – what kind of growing conditions you can provide, and which herbs you are most likely to use. If you have just a few pots on a sunny patio, your choice of herbs may be different from someone with a shady spot or a bigger garden. You will find detailed information on individual herbs throughout the book.

Annual herbs – like chervil, purslane, dill and coriander/cilantro – as well as the salad herbs – like rocket/arugula, mizuna, cress and mustards – are sown each year, and I collect the seeds from one year for growing the next crop. There are two important sowing times. By planting the seeds in mid-spring and then in late summer, I have a year-round supply of these herbs and salad herbs in my kitchen. It is that simple. The salad herbs grow particularly well through the winter months, when their green, maroon and golden leaves of different shapes brighten up my salads.

Perennial herbs will last for decades if they are planted where they have the right soil, the right position in sun or shade and are pruned at the right time of year, which is normally after flowering. Many of them, like thyme, marjoram, hyssop, rosemary, sage, bay and other Mediterranean herbs, need sun and free-draining soil. Only a few like rich soil, damp conditions or shade. But herbs are easy going and my 150 different culinary plants cope well in the sheltered, dry and mainly sunny herb garden.

I have been nurturing the same perennial herb plants for over 20 years since I first put them in the garden. By cutting back after flowering, the different sages, the rosemary, the chives, the sorrel and the lovage, for example, have been thriving for two decades without replacements. They rarely need any attention, like watering or feeding with fertilizers. This is gardening at its simplest and most satisfying.

GROWING IN CONTAINERS

All herbs, annuals and perennials, can be grown in containers, where they like a loam-based soil or compost with extra grit added to improve drainage. As herbs dislike being waterlogged in winter, using porous terracotta pots will also help.

The lifespan of herbs grown in containers is shorter than plants grown in a garden, but you can encourage their survival by feeding and dividing the plants, keeping only the vigorously growing parts of the roots. Protect them in the winter because they are more vulnerable to frost damage than herbs planted in the ground.

Growing in pots curbs the wandering tendencies of vigorous species like mint, which is essential for so many recipes. If I had to choose one mint to grow it would be Bowles's mint because it is good for mint sauce, herb tea and serving with desserts. Some people plant mint in a

large pot, then sink that into the ground to stop the roots from spreading too far.

The other herbs I recommend growing in pots, if there is no garden, include my favourites, lovage and sorrel, which are impossible to find in supermarkets. Good garden centres, however, sell these plants, which survive for years. I would also grow thyme, oregano, rosemary and sage, which all prefer free-draining soil in the sun. If you have space, grow chervil from seed every year because, unlike basil and coriander/cilantro, it is hard to find in food shops.

My other favourite "five-star" herbs are tarragon, chives, bay, dill, parsley and mixed salad herbs. Salad herbs can be bought on a small scale in one seed packet to grow in pots and window boxes. They should be cut for eating every few days when the leaves are small and tender.

HERBS IN THE FLOWER BORDER

In a small garden, another way of planting a good herb selection is to grow them with herbaceous plants or shrubs in a mixed border. Tall architectural herbs like fennel, lovage and angelica work well at the back of a border. Rosemary and bay can be shaped to add structure. Thyme, chives and parsley are best at the front, and plants like hyssop and marjoram add late-summer colour in mid-border, when most other plants have finished flowering.

When you are thinking about where to place herbs in a mixed garden, you need to consider which plants you already have, what colours you like and what the overall effect should be. You need to think, too, about which herbs need sun and free-draining soil, including all the Mediterranean herbs. Plants like chervil, parsley, coriander/cilantro and chives will thrive in any shade you have in the garden, although they can cope with sunny spots, too. Sorrel, angelica, tarragon and lemon balm like partial shade, while lovage and bergamot prefer rich soil.

YOUR OWN HERB GARDEN

If, like me, you are lucky enough to have plenty of space for your herb garden, once you have thought about the basics, you'll find that extra time spent researching and planning is very worthwhile. Plot out your beds, remembering not to make them too large because ideally herbs should never be more than about 70cm/30in from a path, so they are easy to pick and tend. You may like a free-and-easy design or something more formal, which suits herbs well.

In my traditional garden, all the herb beds have a living edge to give definition, using plants like parsley, chives, salad burnet, sorrel, alpine strawberries, primroses and violets. I also use low, trimmed hedges of winter savory and wall germander. Thyme, rosemary, rock hyssop, lavender and small box can also be used. Buy plants young to produce compact hedges which do not become leggy. Planting clipped evergreen herbs to make geometric shapes, called knot gardens, was first recorded in the 15th century. And they are enjoying a resurgence of interest today.

As with flower beds, height is important in the design of formal areas. *Rosa mundi*, a sport, or genetic mutation, from the Apothecary's Rose, is planted in the middle of my beds, providing not only structure but also masses of deep-pink striped petals for recipes like Rose Petal Jam (see page 104). Each one is surrounded by mounds of lemon balm, alternating with showy garlic chives.

The beds are filled with Mediterranean herbs like marjorams, thymes, hyssops and sages. These drought-lovers make the finest of garden plants because many of them keep their leaves all year, so they always look good. Eye-catching herbs also include rosemary shaped into standards, as well as fans on south-facing walls. Different sages are used as full stops at the corners of the beds, while savory hedges are valuable as a framework.

THE PERFECT GARDEN

In the past, herbs played a bigger part in our lives than they do today, whether you lived in a monastery with a formal herb garden, used them in your kitchen or watched the trusted village herbalist or witch concocting potions for sick patients. John Evelyn, the 17th-century writer and gardener, explained all the important herbs to grow. His list was almost as long as the collection of over 150 culinary herbs I grow today. It seems to have been the Victorians who destroyed the love of herbs in Britain with their plain, dull food, while many other parts of the world remained more loyal to their traditional herbs.

My chamomile seat under a rose and jasmine arch is the perfect, scented place to rest, enjoy the colours and aromas in my garden and think about the future for herbs. I often wonder what else I can do to encourage a revival of interest in using these miraculous plants to transform the taste of our food around the world.

SPRING

SPRING HERBS

Like fair-weather gardeners, many perennial herbs hibernate in the cold winter months. But now they are both bravely pushing through the soil and there are new signs of fresh, lively herbs appearing every day. Chives and sweet cicely often make their debut in late winter, but they are soon joined by fennel, lovage and wild rocket/arugula and then mint, bergamot, angelica, lemon balm, buckler-leaf sorrel, garlic chives and savory. The salad herbs sown in late summer are still going strong, but I sow new seeds outside in mid-spring to guarantee a year-round supply. I find spring the most inspiring season in the herb garden.

Fresh, young chives encourage me to make Borscht (see page 30) and I serve this beetroot/beet soup with a blob of sour cream and snipped chives scattered on top. I also make vichyssoise at this time of the year and serve it cold with snipped young chives to give it even more flavour. I make wine vinegar with fresh leaves of salad burnet (see page 147). The Victorians loved the cucumber taste of this vinegar and I make a burnet salad, using the salad burnet vinegar to make the dressing. I also make wine vinegar with the chervil that is still so perfect after the winter months. Chervil vinegar tastes much like its more famous rival tarragon vinegar, so it is a very useful addition in the kitchen.

Spring is the busiest season in the herb garden. There is so much to do, including sowing annual herbs like dill, summer savory and coriander/cilantro, as well as planting some herb seeds in trays in the greenhouse to provide earlier crops. Why buy expensive, pre-packed leaves in "modified atmosphere" packaging that can strip out their vitamins, when they can be simply grown at home in the garden, on the windowsill or in pots and troughs? To achieve a mixture of leaf flavour, colour and texture, I grow a number of salad herbs. But you can buy a similar mix in one seed packet to make it easy to have a variety of tastes in a pot or window box, available to eat as you need them.

I sow salad herbs like rocket/arugula, purslane, Greek cress, basil, American land cress, red orach, lamb's lettuce/corn salad, endive and chicory, mizuna, mibuna and mustards like Red Giant, Golden Streaks and Red Frills, planting them in a pattern of circles, triangles and straight lines to make the salad herb bed look interesting. In four to six weeks the leaves come through the soil. They are picked very young and by pinching off the lower leaves, leaving a rosette of a few small leaves in the middle, the herbs are ready to harvest again after a few days. These annuals also last longer treated this way.

When I started cooking in the 1960s, recipes were rich and rarely used anything green. Now herbs and leaves are the stars on our plates, with their looks, taste and healthy properties. I don't go as far as the late Christopher Lloyd, the great gardener and cook at Great Dixter, East Sussex, southern England, who once served 27 different leaves in one salad. But I am getting close.

Edible flowers also make salads look special and in spring I use violets and primroses in salads, with fresh lovage leaves. I sow viola Heartsease, nasturtium, anchusa, and the marigold *Calendula officinalis* in the greenhouse. But borage – both blue and white flowered – always self-seeds all over the herb garden. Like unruly young children it can get out of control, popping up, full of energy, in every gap. The exquisite flowers decorate food and ice cubes, and the leaves make a chilled Borage and Cucumber Soup (see page 85). I like to try new ideas every year. Last spring I sowed Japanese chrysanthemum, Shungiku, for the first time, enjoying its edible flowers and leaves. This year several new flowers and herbs get a trial.

Seeds are sown outside 5cm/2in apart, in drills about 15cm/6in wide. They are covered with fine soil and a little organic fertilizer. Modules are used in the greenhouse to reduce the need for thinning out and the risk of damaging delicate roots. For a succession of herbs throughout the season, a few seeds are sown every month until late summer when all the salad herbs are sown again, to use throughout the winter. During the colder months, the leaves are never full of holes from the flea beetle and they do not bolt quickly, both of which can happen in spring and summer.

There are many other spring jobs. Herbs like sage, winter savory, bay and thyme need to be tidied up. Cut back old woody shoots and straggly growth, then feed the plants and they will soon freshen up. Rosemary should be pruned after its flowers fade and I like to use some of the cuttings on the log fire to scent the house while the younger shoots are saved to make rosemary syrup, (see page 213) which I use in many cakes and puddings.

This is also a good time to divide herbs like sorrel, lemon balm, lovage and marjoram. I lift and divide my chives every three to four years. Most of them grow around the small pond in the middle of the herb garden, but they also edge a bed in another area, so those can be used for cutting when the pond circle of chives are left to flower.

The hardy common sage, purple, golden and white sages grow outside all year round. But the half-hardy tricolour, pineapple, tangerine and blackcurrant sages are grown in pots because they have to over-winter inside. Just before bringing them out into the garden after the danger of frosts has past, I shape and feed them, as well as splitting plants when necessary.

Herb lovers look forward to late spring when the garden is full of fresh, new luscious leaves and everything looks and tastes wonderful. When Rick Stein wanted to film my herb garden and cooking for his BBC show *Food Heroes*, I asked him to come at this perfect time, when garden was full of edible herbs thriving in the late spring sunshine.

[SPRING ACTION LIST]

+ Divide herbs like lemon balm, sorrel, lovage and chives when necessary.
+ Take root cuttings of sweet cicely, tarragon, mint and bergamot.
+ Layer old, woody herbs like sage and thyme underground to produce new plants.
+ Cut back bay and rosemary; shape other evergreen herbs.
+ Prick out herb seedlings, pot on and eventually harden off.

BASIL

Basil is often called the king of herbs, based on the Greek word for monarch. The French also refer to it as *herbe royale*. And most keen cooks would agree that it is a leader amongst herbs for its fragrance, charisma and addictive taste. It is synonymous with visions of sun-baked Mediterranean landscapes, but is in fact used in recipes from around the world. It is famously eaten in France with tomatoes and mozzarella, mixed with Parmesan cheese and pine nuts in Italian pesto, and used as a vital element in Thai cooking.

HISTORY

This important herb originated in India, where it is still grown around temples and is held sacred to the Hindu gods, Vishnu and Krishna. Basil was put into the hands of the dead to hopefully guarantee a safe journey to the afterlife. In the same way, in Ancient Greece and Ancient Rome, it was thought to open the gates of heaven. Greeks also marked the end of the year by offering basil to the naiads, the spirits of the springs, to ask for a constant supply of natural water in the year ahead.

COOKING

I grow at least three types of basil to cover the variety of tastes needed for recipes from all over the world. The most important, the classic sweet basil, Sweet Genovase, has large, bright green, strongly aromatic leaves and is the variety most often sold in greengrocers and supermarkets. I also grow purple basil for its looks and taste, but the purple basils have less strongly flavoured leaves than the green varieties. Thai basil, including Holy Basil and Queen of Siam, is grown for its very different aniseed scent and flavour. I can also recommend ginger basil, cinnamon basil, anise basil, Greek basil and lemon basil for cooking.

There is no pesto as wonderful as the one I make with my home-grown sweet basil, quality olive oil, Parmesan, pecorino and pine nuts (see page 35). I always have a plant in a pot by the cooker, buying it in the winter months when it is too cold to grow basil easily at home. It is used in many of the recipes in this book. It has a fabulous pungency, but if you cook it, the flavour soon fades away. There is much debate about whether you should avoid cutting basil with a knife. I was taught to tear it into pieces before adding it to a dish after cooking. But recent tests show that the taste and the scent of the leaves is the same, chopped or torn.

Add basil leaves to salads, aubergine/eggplant dishes, courgettes/zucchini and peppers, as well as tomatoes, of course. You can use it with lemon to stuff fish, toss it into pasta with feta cheese, or add one of the Thai basils to spicy soups, cold noodle salads and Thai curries. Introduce the chopped or torn leaves to dishes towards the end of cooking. In some areas, Thai basils can only be bought in oriental supermarkets so it is a good idea to grow your own. Ideally, try to pick your basil leaves for dinner at the end of the day when the flavour of the leaves is more intense.

GROWING

I start to sow basil seeds inside in late winter, using seed compost in trays and encouraging germination by using a heated propagator. The seedlings appear after about a week, and soon after that the first true leaves appear. Then I plant two or three seedlings into each pot and move them out of the propagator and onto the greenhouse shelves. But you can be successful growing basil without a greenhouse. Lots of people sow basil in pots on their windowsills.

It is important to water the plants in the morning or the hottest part of the day, so they are not sitting in wet compost at night when temperatures are lower. If they are wet and cold they can succumb to disease.

Basil is very sensitive to cold weather, so wait until late spring before planting it outside in a warm, sheltered spot. When it is growing strongly you can harvest the basil. Pinch out the main stem to encourage the growth of side shoots. Pinching out the tips will also prevent flowering, which is important because some flavour is lost if the plant runs to seed. Feed weekly with a liquid fertilizer. Basil seeds can also be sown directly into the garden in early summer.

BASIL

BASIL, BORAGE, GORGONZOLA AND FIGS

This is a beautiful dish, made even better if you use both green and purple basil and borage flowers to lift the taste and enhance the beauty of the purple figs. Although I grow blue and white flowered borage, it is the blue flowers with the purple tinge that look so good with this recipe. They are the simplest of herbs to grow, self-seeding every year. You can make this recipe with just the common green basil sold in many shops, but purple basil adds to the glamour of the plate. This basil will grow in pots on the kitchen windowsill and once the weather warms up in late spring, it is easy to grow all basil plants in the garden. Blue cheese goes well with the taste of figs, but never use so much that you overpower the plate.

8 fresh purple figs, washed and
   quartered
115g/4oz Gorgonzola or other
   blue cheese, crumbled
1 small handful of green basil,
   leaves picked
1 small handful of purple basil,
   leaves picked
3 tbsp olive oil
juice of 1 lemon
½ tbsp balsamic vinegar
16 blue-purple borage flowers
sea salt and freshly ground
   black pepper

Arrange 8 pieces of fig on each plate with the Gorgonzola. Scatter over equal amounts of the green and purple basil leaves, then season with salt and pepper to taste.

Mix together the oil, lemon juice and balsamic vinegar. Pour over each plate and finally sprinkle each plate with the borage flowers.

Serves 4

Preparation: 15 mins

COURGETTE, HERB AND GARLIC BRUSCHETTA

The combination of chopped courgette/zucchini, herbs and garlic cooked in a good-quality olive oil is irresistible to me. You can also eat this bruschetta topping with pasta and Parmesan cheese instead of the bread. Basil is important in this recipe, but you can add any other favourite herbs that are not too dominant in taste. Keep the number down to three or the flavours will compete too much. If you don't use the ham, it makes a perfect vegetarian lunch.

3 tbsp olive oil, plus extra for drizzling
1kg/2lb 4oz small, firm courgettes/zucchini, sliced
2 garlic cloves, finely chopped
3 tbsp chopped basil leaves
½ tbsp chopped mint leaves
2 tbsp chopped oregano leaves
4 slices of sourdough bread
8 slices of Serrano or Parma ham/prosciutto
grated zest of ½ lemon (optional)
sea salt and freshly ground black pepper

Heat the oil in a frying pan over a very high heat and fry the courgettes/zucchini for about 5 minutes until they start to brown. Add the garlic and fry for 2 minutes until softened. Add the chopped herbs and season with salt and pepper.

Grill/broil the bread on both sides, then drizzle with oil. Spoon the courgette/zucchini and herb mixture onto the bread, then roll the ham and arrange attractively on top. Sprinkle with the lemon zest, if using.

Serves 4
Preparation: 10 mins
Cooking: 12 mins

BASIL AND TOMATO SORBET

This is perfect for serving as a refreshing appetizer before the main course.

400g/14oz ripe tasty tomatoes
a small handful of basil, plus extra leaves to decorate
1 tsp sugar (optional)
2 egg whites
sea salt and freshly ground black pepper

To remove the skin from the tomatoes, cut a cross in the skin of each tomato at the base with a sharp knife, then put them in a heatproof bowl and cover with boiling water. Leave to stand for 2–3 minutes, or until the skins split, then drain, dip in cold water and drain again. Peel off and discard the skins, deseed the tomatoes and chop the flesh.

Purée the tomatoes with the basil, and season with salt and pepper. Use the sugar only if the purée does not taste sweet enough. Freeze the mixture until it is almost frozen, which will take about 30 minutes in an ice cream machine or 1–2 hours in the freezer.

Whisk the egg whites until stiff, then fold them into the tomato and basil mixture and return to the freezer until completely frozen. Serve a sphere of the sorbet, decorated with whole basil leaves, on a small white dish for each person.

Serves 4

Preparation: 10 mins, plus freezing

CHICKEN BREASTS STUFFED WITH MOZZARELLA AND BASIL

This delicious dish takes only 15 minutes to prepare, and it can all be done in advance to make dinner easier. You need some Classic Pesto made with basil on hand, from my recipe on page 35.

125g/4½oz mozzarella cheese, sliced
4 skinless chicken breasts
24 basil leaves
4 slices of Parma ham/ prosciutto
24 small vine tomatoes
2 tbsp olive oil
450g/1lb small new potatoes
3 tbsp Classic Pesto made with basil (see page 35)
2 tbsp balsamic glaze
sea salt and freshly ground black pepper

Preheat the oven to 190°C/375°F/Gas 5 and grease a baking sheet.

Season the mozzarella with salt and pepper. Make a small pocket in each chicken breast and fill each one with a quarter of the mozzarella and 6 basil leaves. Wrap each chicken breast in a slice of Parma ham, put on the prepared baking sheet and add the vine tomatoes. Drizzle both tomatoes and chicken with the oil and season with salt and pepper. Roast for 20 minutes until the chicken is cooked through.

Meanwhile, boil the potatoes for about 15 minutes, depending on size, until cooked through. Drain, then toss with the basil pesto.

Divide the chicken, pesto potatoes and tomatoes among serving plates and drizzle the tomatoes with the balsamic glaze.

Serves 4

Preparation: 15 mins
Cooking: 20 mins

SMOKED SALMON PASTA WITH SAUCE VIÈRGE

The refreshing sauce is one of my favourites and I often serve this dish as a first course for a special occasion. I also like to serve scallops on a pool of this sauce, or meaty fish like tuna or red mullet, which are improved by the combination of the herbs and the lemony sharpness. Use the black-and-cream-striped bow-shaped pasta for this recipe, if you can find it. It is known as *farfalle zebra* and is made black by the addition of squid ink. I last served this to my American god-daughter and her family who call it "bow-tie pasta". Our grandchildren call it "butterfly pasta", little knowing that *farfalle* is the Italian word for butterfly.

2 ripe tomatoes
75ml/2½fl oz/5 tbsp olive oil
1 shallot, finely chopped
3 tbsp lemon juice
12 coriander seeds, crushed
400g/14oz/6 cups farfalle pasta
16 large basil leaves, finely
  chopped, plus extra leaves
  to serve
16 large coriander/cilantro
  leaves, finely chopped
1 tsp balsamic vinegar
300g/10½oz smoked salmon,
  cut into strips
sea salt and freshly ground
  black pepper

With a sharp knife, cut a cross in the skin of each tomato at the base, then put them in a heatproof bowl and cover with boiling water. Leave to stand for 2–3 minutes, or until the skins split, then drain, dip in cold water and drain again. Peel off and discard the skins, deseed the tomatoes and finely chop the flesh.

Heat 1 tablespoon of the oil in a frying pan and fry the shallot gently for about 10 minutes until softened. Add the rest of the oil, the lemon juice and crushed coriander seeds and heat gently. Then add the tomatoes and heat through.

Meanwhile, cook the farfalle pasta in boiling, salted water for 5–6 minutes, or until al dente.

Just before serving, season the tomato mixture with salt and pepper and add the herbs, then the balsamic vinegar. Cover and leave to rest while you drain the pasta and fold in the strips of smoked salmon. Arrange on serving plates, pour the sauce over the top and sprinkle with a few extra basil leaves.

Preparation: 15 mins
Cooking: 15 mins

Serves 4

CHIVES

I love to see snowdrops appearing, the first flowers of winter. And in just the same way, I celebrate when I realize that brave chives are pushing through the soil, the first fresh herbs to be ready for picking. These hardy perennials from the onion family are easy to grow and essential for cooking. No garden should be without them. There are four types worth growing: the common *Allium schoenoprasum* with its pinky-purple globular flowers and cylindrical leaves; a white-flowered relative; chives with finer leaves; and the taller, bolder garlic chives, also known as Chinese chives, which, unlike the others, have flat, solid leaves.

HISTORY

Chives are one of the most ancient of herbs, with records of their use going back over 5000 years. The Romans believed that eating this herb could increase blood pressure and Romanian gypsies used chives as part of their fortune-telling ritual. Bunches of chives were also hung around houses to ward off both disease and evil.

Chives have been cultivated in Europe since the Middle Ages, playing an important part in many recipes. Their fame spread after reports from Marco Polo, as Europeans took his advice and started using them from the 16th century. They are an essential part of the famous French blend of herbs, *fines herbes*, combined with parsley and tarragon or chervil.

COOKING

Snip chives with scissors to add a mild onion-scented carpet of green to soups and salads. They are wonderful in an omelette (see page 32), but do pop in some chive flowers or buds to the mix when you have them in the garden. Also use them in smoked fish pâtés, potato salads and beetroot/beet dishes. I often make a herb tart with chives and cream cheese. Chive butter can be stored in the refrigerator or freezer. While the smaller chives are soft herbs, which need to be added towards the end of cooking or sprinkled over the final dish, Chinese chives are much tougher. They can be used in dishes at an earlier stage of cooking and can also be stir-fried.

GROWING

Chinese chives grow to 40cm/16in high and have a sweet garlic flavour and large white flowers all summer, which also look good in the winter when they have dried on the stem. Because they are so showy, I grow them in six clumps around the roses in the middle of my herb beds. The clumps of garlic chives alternate with six clumps of variegated lemon balm, which together make an attractive circle because the strappy leaves of the chives contrast so well with the colourful, rounded lemon balm leaves.

You can grow chives from seed in late spring, but I usually just split the clumps to increase their numbers. If you want to grow chives in clumps, plant about six bulbs together roughly 15cm/6in away from the next clump. I grow most of mine as edging plants around my herb beds, planting them in close rows of one bulb width, about 10cm/4in from the edge of the bed. When they are refreshed with compost and water, the plants soon thicken up.

Chives will grow almost anywhere, but they like sun and rich soil and the leaves can go yellow if they are not happy. When you grow them in pots or a window box you will need to give them a liquid feed and keep them well watered. Many gardeners plant them with their vegetables and roses because they are thought to reduce diseases like black spot. Chives thrive by being cut back to 2.5cm/1in from the ground about four times a year to encourage fresh, green growth. They should always be cut back after flowering.

When winter is on the way, I usually dig up a clump to grow in the greenhouse, which I also do with tarragon and some mints, as these herbs disappear under the ground in cold weather. I also snip the fresh chive leaves finely and keep them in the freezer in an ice-cube tray with water. Another way to enjoy the taste of chives in the winter is to make white wine vinegar flavoured with the leaves and buds (see page 147). Preserved or freshly picked, chives have an essential role in my kitchen.

BORSCHT WITH SOUR CREAM AND CHIVES

Beetroot/beet is a big favourite in my household and we cook this wonderful vegetable in many ways. Borscht is always welcome, particularly when I scatter it with snipped chives and chive flowers if it is the time of year when the flowers are at their best.

1 large onion, chopped
1 tbsp olive oil
1 garlic clove, finely chopped
2 cooked beetroots/beets, peeled and grated
800ml/28fl oz/3⅓ cups chicken stock
125ml/4floz/½ cup sour cream
1 small handful of chives, finely snipped
4 pink chive flowers (optional)
sea salt and freshly ground black pepper

Fry the onion in the oil in a large saucepan for about 10 minutes until softened. Add the garlic and continue to fry for a few minutes. Add the grated beetroots/beets and stock and season with salt and pepper. Simmer gently for about 10 minutes until the stock is coloured and well flavoured with the beetroot/beet. Be careful not to overcook.

Blend the soup, then rub through a sieve/fine-mesh strainer. Serve with a swirl of sour cream in each bowl, the snipped chives scattered on the surface and a chive flower in the middle of the sour cream, if using.

Serves 4

Preparation: 20 mins
Cooking: 30 mins

ASPARAGUS WITH CHIVE MAYONNAISE

Asparagus served with chive mayonnaise is a magical combination. The best way to make mayonnaise is by hand as it produces a softer texture. Using a machine to do the job seems to toughen the protein in the egg yolks, leaving you with a stiff end product. My husband likes to make mayonnaise, so he has become the expert in our kitchen. He always makes sure that all ingredients are at room temperature before he starts.

900g/2lb asparagus

CHIVE MAYONNAISE
2 egg yolks
2 tsp white wine vinegar
a pinch of salt
300ml/10fl oz/1¼ cups best-quality extra
   virgin olive oil
2 tbsp finely snipped chives

To make the mayonnaise, combine the egg yolks, vinegar and salt in a bowl. Gradually beat the oil into the mixture, adding just a tiny bit at a time at first until the mixture begins to thicken up. If you add the oil too quickly, it can curdle, so be patient. Once all the oil is incorporated, you should have a thick, glossy mayonnaise.

To prepare and cook the asparagus, cut off the woody base end of each stalk. Steam the asparagus for 5–10 minutes until it is tender, depending on the thickness of the stems. Drain and divide among serving plates. At the last minute, stir the chives into the mayonnaise and serve.

Serves 4
Preparation: 15 mins
Cooking: 10 mins

CHIVE FLOWER OMELETTE

The pink-purple tufted flowers of the chive plant taste delicately of onion and make food look beautiful too. You can also use this recipe to make a classic omelette *fines herbes*, adding tarragon and parsley to the eggs along with the chives, and omitting the chive flowers.

8 eggs
4 tbsp milk
1 tbsp finely snipped chives
1 tbsp butter
16 chive flowers
sea salt and freshly ground black pepper

Beat together the eggs and milk, add the chives and season with salt and pepper.

Melt the butter in a large frying pan until foaming, pour in the omelette mixture and cook for about 5 minutes until it is set but still moist. Scatter the chive flowers over the top, then flip it over and cook for a further 1 minute, keeping it soft and moist.

Divide the omelette into four, flipping the pieces back over so that the flowers are on the top. Slide onto warm plates to serve.

Serves 4

Preparation: 10 mins
Cooking: 10 mins

COD WITH A SOY AND CHIVE MARINADE

This recipe is one of my favourites and I have been serving it for decades. The combined flavour of sesame oil and soy sauce is perfect with chives, ginger and spring onions/scallions. The sauce has a refreshing taste, which also works well with chicken.

4 cod fillets, or fillets of another
   meaty fish such as halibut
2 tbsp sesame oil
3 tbsp soy sauce
4 tbsp snipped chives
2 bay leaves
6 spring onions/scallions,
   chopped
1 large garlic clove, finely sliced
2.5cm/1in cube of root ginger,
   finely sliced or grated
sea salt and freshly ground
   black pepper

Rub the cod on each side with half the sesame oil, then put in a non-metallic bowl. Toss with half the soy sauce, half the chives and the bay leaves, then cover and leave to marinate in the refrigerator for at least 2 hours.

Preheat the grill/broiler to high. Heat the remaining sesame oil in a frying pan and fry half the spring onions/scallions with the garlic and ginger for about 10 minutes until softened. Add pepper, then taste to check whether salt is needed – it may not be because the soy is salty. Meanwhile, grill/broil the fillets for about 10–15 minutes until the fish flakes easily when tested with a fork.

Spoon the marinade over the top of the fish, then sprinkle with the remaining spring onions/scallions and chives to serve, with the remaining soy sauce alongside.

Serves 4

Preparation: 15 mins, plus marinating
Cooking: 15 mins

HERB PESTO

When herbs are abundant and at their best, make lots of pesto, putting some into
the freezer in small plastic pots or ice cube trays. Give jars away to friends, pouring
a little olive oil over the surface of the pesto to seal it and stop it going brown.

Pesto is the prince of Italian dishes. Making it is a pleasure as the fragrance fills the air and stimulates the appetite. Originating in Genoa, the capital of Liguria, the name means "to pound", because the ingredients are ground in the mortar by the circular motion of the pestle.

There are two predecessors to pesto. The Ancient Romans ate a similar paste, called *moretum*, which included the normal garlic, herbs, olive oil and cheese, but also had vinegar added. In the Middle Ages a paste was made by Italians called *agliata*, which contains garlic and walnuts. In Sicily, pesto is made using almonds.

Basil did not make its entrance until the mid 19th century, when pesto as we know it became popular. Genoa is most famous for this sauce but every family in every town has its own version. Some add a few tablespoons of ricotta to soften the taste. You can get the same effect by adding fromage frais. It is often served on squares of pasta in Italy, called "silk handkerchiefs". Potatoes and string beans are traditionally added and the dish is finished with pesto.

The traditional way to pound your pesto is to use a pestle and mortar. Competitions for the best pesto are held in Italy every year and everyone has to make their contribution in this old-fashioned way. I own 26 different pestle and mortars, collected all over the world, the smallest in brass found within the old city

walls in Jerusalem and the largest, over 30cm/12in tall, roughly hewn from a tree trunk in Kenya.

My favourite, which I use almost every day, was made of rough pottery in a refugee camp for the Karen tribe on the Burma/Thailand border. I was filming, with the BBC, the World Health Organization's first trials of using the herb artemisia to treat malaria patients in a hospital set up there by *Medecins sans Frontières*. We all slept on the floor – patients, doctors and film crew alike. The mosquitoes were biting, the rats and scorpions were scavenging, the temperatures were high and the producer felt sorry for me having to report the science to camera for a few hours every day without getting much sleep. The pestle and mortar were his way of saying thank you and every time I use it I think of those patients and the great results of the trial. Artemisia has now successfully treated millions of patients worldwide.

I make several types of pesto at my herb cookery classes, including favourites like rocket/arugula or lovage, which are superb. I also like pesto made from sage, wild garlic leaves, coriander/cilantro and parsley. I use pine nuts for pesto made from more subtle herbs, but walnuts are best for recipes using stronger herbs, such as lovage, sage, rocket/arugula and wild garlic. Parmesan is saltier and less subtle than pecorino. It is worth going to the effort of using both in my Classic Pesto. But for simplicity I usually only use Parmesan in other pesto recipes.

CLASSIC PESTO

I sometimes make small amounts of pesto using the pestle and mortar, although my food processor does most of the work. Do not blend the mix for too long as the pesto needs to have a rough texture.

2 handfuls of basil, or other delicate herbs such as
   parsley, chervil or coriander/cilantro
1 garlic clove
3 tbsp pine nuts, toasted
100ml/3½fl oz/scant ½ cup extra virgin olive oil
4 tbsp freshly grated Parmesan cheese
4 tbsp freshly grated pecorino
freshly ground black pepper

Start by blending the basil with the garlic and then the toasted pine nuts – they thicken the pesto and add to the richness. Then very slowly add the olive oil until well blended and finally stir in the grated cheese and season with pepper.

Makes about 240ml/8fl oz/1 cup
Preparation: 15 mins

STRONG HERB PESTO

Gutsy, strong flavours like lovage, savory or wild garlic are good for pesto, but I make them with walnuts instead of pine nuts and double the quantity – using 50g/1¾oz walnuts. For obvious reasons, I omit garlic cloves with wild garlic dishes.

1 large garlic clove (omit for wild garlic pesto)
2 handfuls of chosen strong herb, such as sage,
   rocket/arugula, lovage, savory or wild garlic
50g/1¾oz/½ cup walnuts
100ml/3½fl oz/scant ½ cup extra virgin olive oil
8 tbsp freshly grated Parmesan cheese (or half
   Parmesan and half pecorino)
freshly ground black pepper

As in the classic pesto recipe, blend the herb and garlic together, then add the nuts and blend again. Very slowly dribble in the olive oil. Stir in the cheese and season with black pepper.

Makes about 240ml/8fl oz/1 cup
Preparation: 15 mins

SPRING

PESTO TRIANGLES

Mixing pesto with cream cheese makes a perfect filling for these golden pastry triangles. They are my favourite canapés, but for more ideas, see pages 224–5. Any spare sheets of pastry in the packet, left over from the recipe, could be used to make an apple or cherry strudel.

olive oil, for brushing and greasing
1 recipe quantity Strong Herb Pesto made with rocket/arugula, lovage or sage (see page 35)
240g/8oz/1 cup cream cheese
4 sheets of filo/phyllo pastry
freshly grated Parmesan cheese, for sprinkling

Preparation: 30 mins
Cooking: 10 mins

Preheat the oven to 220°C/425°F/Gas 7 and grease a large baking sheet with oil. Take the pastry out of the refrigerator about 20 minutes before you want to use it.

In a small bowl, combine the pesto and cream cheese.

Cut the filo sheets lengthways into 5 strips, each 5 × 34cm/2 × 13½in. Place a heaped teaspoonful of the filling in the corner of the first filo strip, covering the remaining pastry strips with a damp dish towel to prevent them from drying out. Fold the corner of the pastry over the filling to make a triangle. Keep folding the corner, one way then the other, until you are almost at the top. Brush the top with a little oil, then fold into a triangle. Repeat with the remaining strips, then place the pastry triangles on the prepared baking sheet.

Brush the top of each triangle with a little olive oil, and sprinkle a little grated Parmesan over each one. Cook in the preheated oven for 7–10 minutes until golden brown and cooked through.

Makes 20

[WHY NOT TRY...]

+ Stirring a dollop of pesto through minestrone soup
+ Topping a cooked puff pastry base with roasted Mediterranean vegetables and drizzling with pesto for a quick summery tart
+ Adding pesto to a simple tomato sauce to serve with meatballs, for instant flavour
+ Stirring pesto through freshly steamed new potatoes
+ Adding 2–3 teaspoons of pesto to a basic risotto recipe (see page 180)

HERB PESTO

FENNEL

Fennel is a tall and handsome perennial which looks elegant with other herbs or at the back of a mixed flower border. There are green and bronze varieties, but the green herb tastes slightly better. It has a sweetly fragrant liquorice flavour, with a hint of camphor. The seeds are even stronger than the leaves, but are essential to many recipes. Fennel now grows wild in many parts of the world. I never tire of seeing it when I holiday in other countries, swaying on its tall stems topped with all its cheerful yellow flowers.

HISTORY

Fennel is native to the Mediterranean and was used by the Ancient Greeks in herbal medicines for at least 20 different medical conditions. The Romans preferred it in their food, eating leaves, roots and seeds. Roman soldiers also believed that tasty fennel helped maintain their health and strength, keeping them fit for battle. Back at the villas, their women believed it was an appetite suppressant and used it in their slimming regimes. In the Middle Ages, fennel had a less romantic use. Its strong flavour was used to disguise the taste of food that was not as fresh as it should be.

COOKING

It is rare to see fennel fronds on sale in food shops, despite the fact that fennel is an important ingredient in fish dishes and many other recipes. I often use the stalks and leaves to stuff a whole fish before baking, before using finely chopped fennel leaves in fish stock or a sauce to go with the baked fish. I cut the stalks of my fennel to the ground in early winter, but soon have small leaves poking through the ground in the coldest months when dill will not grow. So I often use fennel as a reasonable substitute in dill recipes.

Fennel is particularly good with gamey fish like red mullet (see page 43) and in Sicily it is an essential in their strong-tasting sardine recipes. One favourite recipe is to stuff the fish with fennel, currants and pine nuts. In Britain we seem to prefer a gooseberry and fennel sauce to serve with mackerel. I also use chopped fennel with root vegetables, including new potatoes or beetroot/beet, with shellfish, smoked eel, eggs, tomatoes and to add an aniseed flavour to sour cream or mayonnaise. The seeds are more spicy than the leaves and are important in the kitchen with rich foods like duck, pork and lamb.

The seeds can be rubbed into the meat before cooking, or ground to add to spice mixes used for soups, bread or salad dressings.

At the end of the summer, I chop up fennel leaves finely to add to ice cube trays with water and freeze. And you can dry the fennel stems to use in the winter with olive oil to flavour baked fish. Fennel herb is quite different to the white bulb of Florence fennel. But you will see from my recipe on page 41 that the herb and the root vegetable can be combined successfully.

Travelling in Morocco, I discovered people sitting on the pavement surrounded by dried umbels of fennel, which they sell for a double purpose. The stalks are used as toothpicks and then the seeds are chewed as a breath-freshener. I now serve them after dinner for anyone interested in historic herbal hygiene. I have since found that fennel is used to flavour natural toothpastes and the roasted seeds are used in *mukhwas* – an after-meal digestive and breath-freshener in Pakistan and India.

GROWING

Grow fennel from seed in early spring, well away from dill because they can cross-pollinate. It likes a sunny spot in well-drained soil, but will be happy in a large pot. As with all herbs, you will get more leafy growth if you prevent flowering until later in the summer. Then leave some flowers on the plant and the seeds will soon start to form. You can collect a few seeds to taste when they are young, green and juicy. But leave most of them to turn pale brown and then dry them by hanging them upside down, loosely enclosed in a paper bag. When they are totally dry, store them in an airtight jar. Although fennel is a perennial plant, it usually needs replacing every three to four years.

BAKED FLORENCE FENNEL WITH PARMESAN AND FENNEL BUTTER

This dish combines both types of fennel – the delicious Florence fennel bulb, and the herb fennel leaves. Fennel and Parmesan cheese are a great combination, which I have been using for years. Uncooked fennel bulbs go dry and start to brown very quickly, so blanch them soon after buying or harvesting, and keep in the refrigerator until you want to make this dish.

2–3 Florence fennel bulbs, depending on size
30g/1oz/2 tbsp butter
4 tbsp freshly grated Parmesan cheese
sea salt and freshly ground black pepper

FENNEL BUTTER
175g/6oz/¾ cup butter, softened
2 tbsp lemon juice
3 tbsp chopped herb fennel leaves
1 small garlic clove, crushed

Preheat the oven to 190°C/375°F/Gas 5. Reserve and chop a few of the fennel fronds for the fennel butter. Slice the fennel bulb, then blanch it in boiling water for 2 minutes – it must not become soft. Drain well, then toss it in the butter. Put in an ovenproof dish, scatter with the Parmesan and season with salt and pepper. Cook in the oven for up to 15 minutes until the cheese is turning golden brown.

Meanwhile, make the fennel butter. In a bowl, blend together all the ingredients, including the reserved fennel fronds, and spoon onto a strip of baking parchment. Use the paper to help you shape the herb butter into a long roll, then twist the paper at the ends to seal. Chill until needed, then slice about half the butter into small rounds. (Store the leftover butter in the refrigerator or freezer and use on fish or cooked vegetables.)

Serve the baked fennel topped with slices of the fennel butter.

Serves 4

Preparation: 20 mins
Cooking: 20 mins

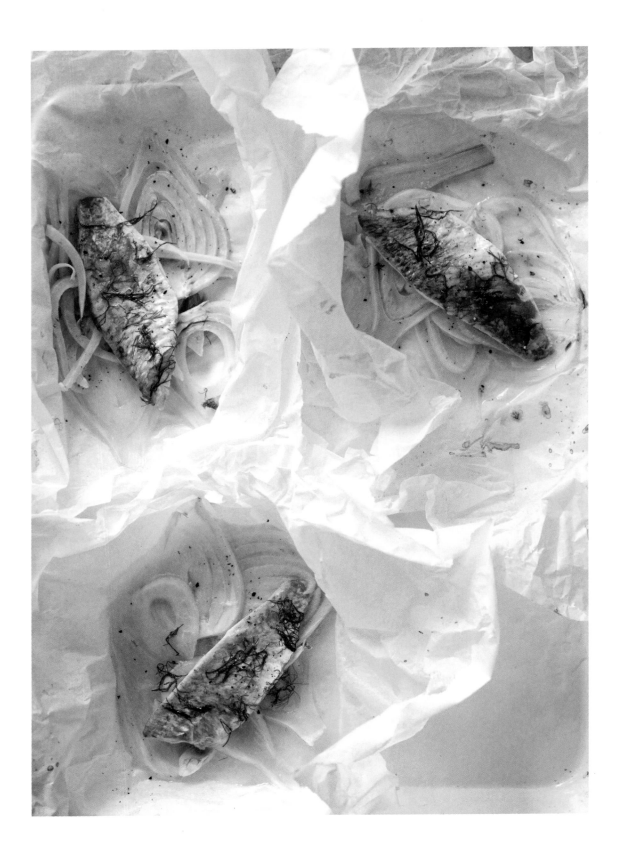

FENNEL, PERNOD AND RED MULLET PARCELS

Fennel and fish make a classic and classy combination, helped by the aniseed flavour of the Pernod. Nothing could be easier than this recipe, in which a foil or baking parchment parcel holds in all the wonderful flavours and cooking juices. Do take care when opening the parcels as they will trap a lot of hot steam inside.

2 Florence fennel bulbs

2 tbsp chopped herb fennel leaves

1 glass of dry white wine, about 180ml/6fl oz/¾ cup

2 tbsp Pernod

1 tbsp butter

4 fillets of red mullet, sea bass or another favourite fish

sea salt and freshly ground black pepper

Preheat the oven to 190°C/375°F/Gas 5. Reserve and chop a few of the fennel fronds. Thinly slice the fennel bulb.

Prepare four 30cm/12in squares of double-thickness baking parchment or kitchen foil. Divide the ingredients equally among the parchment squares, placing the fish fillets on top. Season with salt and pepper. Fold the foil in half and twist the edges together to seal, keeping some air inside. Bake for about 15 minutes until the fish flakes easily when tested with a fork.

Serve in the baking parchment parcels or, if you prefer, you can open the parcels and arrange the fish, fennel and sauce on serving plates.

Serves 4

Preparation: 10 mins
Cooking: 15 mins

LEMON VERBENA

Lemon verbena – with its light green, elongated leaves and beautiful pale mauve flowers – looks elegantly ornamental in the large pot where it grows in my herb garden. But when it comes to tasting it, the herb's personality changes, because it packs a powerful punch of both lemon juice and zest. I think this is the most important of all lemon-flavoured plants, so I am always surprised that few people use it in the kitchen. It is rarely found on sale as a cut herb, so I strongly recommend that you grow it yourself.

LEMON VERBENA AND APRICOT CLAFOUTIS

HISTORY

The Spanish brought lemon verbena from its native South America to Europe in the 17th century, where it was first used for its scented oil. It took a long time to become known as a culinary herb, but once tasted, it becomes memorable for its intense citrus flavour. This comes mainly from the compound citral, which is also present in lemongrass. Only last week I was preparing Thai hot and sour prawn soup from a recipe which listed lemongrass. Lemon verbena was a perfect substitute.

COOKING

Make lemon verbena syrup (see page 130) to add to fruit or cakes, or try ice cream or sorbet (see pages 110–11), tea (see page 46), apple jelly (see page 166), stuffings and verbena sugar (see page 132). Bruise the leaves to add lemon flavour to drinks, or thread onto skewers when you are cooking fish or meat on the barbecue. For winter use, you can chop the leaves finely and freeze in ice cube trays, or dry the leaves before storing in an airtight container for up to three years.

GROWING

I grow lemon verbena in a pot and bring it inside before the first frosts. But you can grow it outside in a well-drained, sunny and sheltered spot, like by a south-facing wall. It benefits from a mulch and fleece for extra protection in the cold months. This herb loses its leaves in winter, so cut it back before this happens and you will be rewarded with lots of new growth in late spring. It can be grown from seed, but taking cuttings is a more successful way of producing new plants, which should be kept in pots for at least two years. Use liquid fertilizer during the flowering period.

Apricots are one of my favourite fruits and I have been meaning to plant one on a sunny barn wall for some time. But for now I have to buy them and I always try to find ripe fruit which is full of flavour. The zing of lemon verbena leaves lifts this dessert, making it very special indeed. Clafoutis is a favourite dessert from central France, which is also successful with plums or cherries.

30g/1oz/2 tbsp butter, for greasing
500g/1lb 2oz ripe apricots
3 tbsp very finely chopped lemon verbena leaves, plus a sprig to decorate
85g/3oz/scant ½ cup caster/superfine sugar
240ml/8fl oz/1 cup single/light cream
4 eggs
60g/2¼oz/½ cup plain/all-purpose flour
1 tbsp icing/confectioners' sugar, sifted

Preheat the oven to 180°C/350°F/Gas 4 and generously butter a large gratin dish. Cut the apricots in half and remove the pits. Arrange, cut-side down, in the dish and sprinkle the chopped lemon verbena leaves over the top.

Blend the sugar, cream, eggs and flour until smooth, then pour the mixture over the fruit and bake for 30 minutes until the clafoutis is puffed up and lightly browned. Serve warm, but not hot, sprinkled with icing/confectioners' sugar and decorated with a sprig of lemon verbena.

Serves 4–6

Preparation: 25 mins
Cooking: 30 mins

HERB TEAS

My gardening trainee, Alan, told me recently about the tisane trolley used in the restaurant where he worked, with its vast selection of fresh and dried herb teas. This struck me as an excellent idea because more and more people are getting fussy about the types of coffee and more traditional teas that they will swallow. But however fussy my visitors are, they rarely turn down herb tea.

I always make tea with fresh herbs, either straight into a china cup or mug, in a glass herb tea pot or *tisanière*, with the central container for the herb, or in a cafetière. Fleshy-leaved herbs should be washed and torn before handfuls are put in the base of the coffee maker. Then boil the water and leave for a minute before pouring. Allow to infuse for several minutes, then press down the plunger and pour the tea. Never use boiling water because it will scald the herbs and damage the flavour.

I do not add sugar, but many people think it enhances the flavour. I remember drinking mint tea for the first time in Morrocco and thinking the very sweet tea tasted horribly like the unsubtle chewing gum I used to buy as a child. But there is little more refreshing than a herb tea, sweet or not, served mid-morning, for afternoon tea, or after a meal. It is easy, tasty and caffeine-free – and you know that no chemicals have been used in processing.

It is important to be generous with the quantity of soft herbs used. But do not follow the rule with hard herbs like rosemary. This makes a good winter tea, but never put more than one small sprig per cup as it is so strong. With many other herbs I would average 3 sprigs per cup, and about 12 in a *tisanière*. You can cool and chill herb tea and serve with ice on a hot day, or spiced with cloves, cinnamon and orange peel in the winter.

Bergamot has citrus minty leaves, which are good served with a lemon slice.

Camomile tea is said to help with insomnia. You need to grow the flowering type of this herb for tea making. Wait until the white petals begin to fold back from the yellow middles. Hang bunches upside down until the herb is dry and brittle. Then make the tea by steeping 1 tsp of the flowers in 200ml/7fl oz/¾ cup of boiled water. Infuse for 5 minutes, strain and sip.

Lemon balm tea is one of my favourites. It is refreshing hot or iced. I have so much of this herb in my garden that I never run out.

Lemon verbena makes perfect, refreshing tea. Many people tell me it helps them to sleep.

Mint tea can be made with a choice of mints. I like Bowles's mint, but also use Moroccan, pineapple, chocolate and ginger mint.

Sage leaves make another strong tea. It is one of the few that I think improves with sugar and lemon.

Thyme tea is said to be good for hangovers, but it is strong, so use the tips of the branches sparingly.

LOVAGE

Lovage is my favourite herb. There is something very special about its spicy, celery flavour and I use it for various dishes almost every day. It is also essential in the hot summer months for shading my greenhouse. As it grows to over 2m/6ft tall with large, lush, deeply divided leaves, I have planted it every 60cm/24in along the south side of my greenhouse so that it helps to keep things cool. Some people call it love parsley, although it looks nothing like any of the parsleys and tastes very different. It is in the Umbelliferae family and as well as the tall version, *Levisticum officinale*, which has yellow flowers and brown seed heads, there is a shorter lovage called *Levisticum scoticum*, with white flowers and a milder flavour. It is a Mediterranean herb which loves the sun and, unusually for many herbs, it enjoys rich soil. So do compost it when it dies down late in the year.

HISTORY

The Ancient Greeks were said to use lovage extensively and the Romans liked to grow it for the seeds, which they chewed to help digestion. People who travelled in the Middle Ages were known to use the leaves as odour-eaters in their shoes and even today the leaves are known for their deodorizing and antiseptic effects. Lovage was planted in medieval monasteries and became a popular, easy to grow herb in Europe for both its flavour and reputation as an aphrodisiac. Today it is largely unknown and hard to buy as a cut herb for cooking. But once people grow their own plants, they usually become addicted, like me, to its spicy, celery flavour with a hint of both lemon and orange.

COOKING

I pick the leaves as soon as they push through the ground in early spring. The fresh, baby leaves are wonderful in salads. As the flavour is good with carrots, I use the leaves in carrot salads and I cook them along with the vegetable, too. Carrot and lovage soup is excellent. In fact, the leaves improve many hearty soups, but the best recipe of all is my simple Lovage Soup made with potatoes (see page 50), which is a family favourite. I cooked it for Rick Stein when he visited my herb garden for his *Food Heroes* BBC TV series.

The combination of courgette/zucchini and lovage also makes a creamy, green soup with an excellent and unusual flavour. When courgette/zucchini plants are running riot, just soften some chopped onion and garlic and add any oversized courgettes/zucchini cut into small pieces, removing the seeds but keeping the skin. Simmer this mixture in some good-quality stock with a handful of lovage leaves, then, once the ingredients have softened, blend the soup until smooth. I often make and freeze lovage soups, along with lovage purée for sauces,

and a gutsy lovage pesto (see page 35). Lovage can be used and cooked like spinach, it makes a memorable sauce with chicken or fish and it combines well with cheese in a soufflé. But my favourite use of lovage is with guinea fowl, a delicious recipe you will find on page 52.

I also store the seeds to use in the kitchen. Lovage seeds are known as *ajwain*, and have a wonderful thymey flavour. One new recipe I have just tried is to rub duck breasts with lovage seeds, ground cumin and chopped chilli, then grill/broil them and serve with a sauce made from the flavoured juices, good-quality stock and red wine. The seeds are also good in biscuits, bread, soups and on rice and salads.

GROWING

The leaves stay green and fresh from early spring through to summer, when first they start to taste bitter and then they go pale and lose their flavour. This is the time to cut the plant back to encourage fresh shoots, which give the plant and my recipes a new lease of life.

Some lovage stems should be left uncut so that they can flower and form seed heads. Unlike lovage seeds, the leaves do not dry successfully for winter use. Once the seeds have turned brown, they can be collected and hung upside down to dry inside a paper bag. In the autumn, these seeds should be planted out in the garden. The young plants will reach full size in three to five years. They are happy growing in a sunny south-facing spot, but will also cope with partial shade.

In early spring I also sow the seeds in trays inside and cover with vermiculite, using a propagator to speed up germination. It is also possible to divide the roots in autumn or spring to produce new plants. Look out for new buds on each root section.

LOVAGE

LOVAGE SOUP WITH CARROT PURÉE

Lovage has a great affinity with carrots and the swirl of carrot purée finishes off this soup beautifully. As an alternative, you can serve the soup with croûtons topped with Strong Herb Pesto made with lovage (see page 35).

1 onion, chopped
2 tbsp olive oil
1 garlic clove, finely chopped
4 floury potatoes, (about
   680g/1lb oz) washed and
   chopped
1 large handful of lovage leaves,
   plus extra to garnish
600ml/21fl oz/2½ cups chicken
   or vegetable stock
sea salt and freshly ground
   black pepper
4 tbsp cream or plain yogurt,
   to serve

CARROT PURÉE
4 carrots, peeled and chopped
3 tbsp vegetable stock

Fry the onion in the oil in a large saucepan for about 10 minutes until softened. Add the garlic and continue to fry for a few minutes. Add the potatoes, lovage leaves and stock and simmer for about 12 minutes in a covered pan until the potatoes are soft. Finely chop the lovage leaves for the garnish.

Meanwhile, cover the carrots with water in a separate pan, bring to the boil and cook for about 10 minutes until soft. Drain and mash, then purée with a few tablespoons of vegetable stock until smooth. Season with salt and pepper.

Blend the lovage soup until smooth, then season with salt and pepper to taste and pour into bowls. Swirl a spoonful of carrot purée and cream into each bowl and sprinkle with the finely chopped lovage leaves to serve.

Serves 4

Preparation: 15 mins
Cooking: 25 mins

VENISON FILLET WITH LOVAGE, CELERY, WALNUTS AND APPLE

I make this recipe for four people using venison fillet steaks, but it can also be a special-occasion dish for a larger number by roasting a haunch of venison. It looks very attractive on the plate surrounded by the lovage, walnuts and diced apple. I often serve this with new potatoes and a green vegetable such as spinach.

200ml/7fl oz/scant 1 cup red wine
1 small handful of lovage, leaves picked and chopped, plus 16 small leaves to serve
1 bay leaf
6 black peppercorns, crushed
2 garlic cloves, chopped
4 venison fillet steaks, about 150g/5½oz each
100ml/3½fl oz/scant ½ cup game or chicken stock
1 tbsp redcurrant jelly, plus extra to serve
2 tbsp olive oil
1 small apple, diced
2 celery stalks, diced
55g/2oz/½ cup walnuts, chopped
30g/1oz/2 tbsp butter
10 celery leaves
sea salt and freshly ground black pepper

Preparation: 20 mins, plus marinating
Cooking: 20 mins

To make the marinade, mix together the wine, lovage leaves, bay leaf, peppercorns and garlic in a non-metallic bowl. Add the venison steaks, cover with cling film/plastic wrap and leave to marinate in the refrigerator for up to 2 days, turning regularly.

Lift the venison out of the marinade, pat dry on paper towels and leave to one side. Pour the marinade through a sieve/fine-mesh strainer into a saucepan, add the stock and boil for several minutes until it starts to thicken. Season with salt and pepper, then add the redcurrant jelly and simmer until the jelly has melted, stirring occasionally. Taste and add more jelly if the flavour is too sharp.

Preheat a griddle pan. Rub the venison steaks with the oil, season with salt and pepper and cook in the griddle pan for about 3 minutes on each side until browned but still pink in the middle. Wrap in foil and leave to rest for several minutes.

Meanwhile, cook the apple, celery and walnuts in the butter for 3 minutes. Add the lovage and celery leaves just before serving.

Unwrap the venison and put a steak in the middle of each plate. Surround with a circle of the mixed celery, apple, walnuts and leaves. Serve with the sauce and a small bowl of redcurrant jelly.

Serves 4

LOVAGE

GUINEA FOWL WITH LOVAGE AND LIME

This recipe is one of my favourites and I have been serving it for decades. It has a memorable flavour, which only lovage can provide, and it can be made for most of the year, except when lovage disappears under the ground in mid-winter. You can serve this with potatoes, carrots cooked with chopped lovage leaves, and extra lime.

1 onion, chopped

1 tbsp olive oil

1 garlic clove, finely chopped

150ml/5fl oz/scant ⅔ cup chicken stock

1 guinea fowl

1 very large handful of lovage, plus extra to serve

3 tbsp dry vermouth

grated zest and juice of 1 lime

120ml/4fl oz/½ cup double/ heavy cream

sea salt and freshly ground black pepper

carrots and boiled or mashed potatoes, to serve

Preheat the oven to 190°C/375°F/Gas 5. Fry the onion in the oil in a large flameproof casserole dish for about 10 minutes until softened. Add the garlic and continue to fry for a few minutes. Add the stock and then the guinea fowl, breast-side down. Lay the lovage on top of the bird. Cover with the lid and cook in the oven for about 25 minutes.

Take out the casserole dish and remove the lid. Lift out and discard the lovage, which will now be dry and crisp and have released its wonderful flavour into the liquid. Turn the guinea fowl over so the breasts are exposed, season with salt and pepper, add the vermouth and lime zest and juice, then return to the oven, uncovered, for another 20 minutes or so until the bird is cooked through and browned.

Remove the bird from the dish and leave it to rest while you finish the sauce. Add the cream to the liquid in the dish and simmer on the hob/stovetop over a medium heat, stirring regularly, until the sauce has thickened. Sprinkle the guinea fowl with lovage leaves and serve with carrots and potatoes with the sauce on the side.

Serves 4

Preparation: 15 mins
Cooking: 1 hr

NECTARINES WITH AMARETTI AND A LOVAGE DRIZZLE

This is one of the simplest recipes ever – so simple that I have given presents of a tin of good amaretti biscuits and a bag of nectarines or peaches to friends, with instructions for this recipe attached. Just as I love giving bunches of herbs away to inspire people to experiment, I also cannot resist encouraging people to cook.

6 just-ripe nectarines or peaches, halved and pitted
12 bite-size amaretti biscuits
175g/6oz/1⅓ cups fresh raspberries or redcurrants (optional)
2 tbsp icing/confectioners' sugar, for dusting, if using the red fruit
a little butter, for greasing

LOVAGE DRIZZLE
1 small handful of lovage leaves, picked and chopped
4 tbsp caster/superfine sugar

Preheat the oven to 180°C/350°F/Gas 4 and grease a baking dish.

Make the lovage drizzle by boiling the lovage and sugar in 150ml/5fl oz/ scant ⅔ cup water until you have a syrup consistency. Blend the mixture in a food processor, then strain through a coffee filter to give a strong, green syrup.

Put the fruit, cut-side up, in the prepared dish. Fill each hollow that has been left by a stone with one amaretti biscuit. Sprinkle with the lovage syrup and cook for 10–15 minutes until the fruit is soft and the amaretti lightly browned. Serve warm or cold.

As this is a sweet dish, you can serve it with the sharp red fruit dusted with icing/confectioners' sugar. It is a good combination for taste and looks. Serve each person three nectarine halves surrounded on the dish with red fruit, if you are using them.

Serves 4

Preparation: 15 mins
Cooking: 25 mins

MINT

Mint's refreshing, clean taste is vital to many dishes, both savoury and sweet. It looks good both on the plate and in the garden. But when you buy it as a bunch of leaves, it can be disappointing, so always try to grow some in your garden or in a pot kept in the kitchen if you have no outdoor space. The leaves can be picked fresh from spring to early winter, but they are at their best before flowering. When the flowers do appear, pick them too, because they have a wonderful mint taste and can be added to salads and summer fruit recipes.

HISTORY

The botanical name *Mentha* is thought to have come from Ancient Greek mythology. Hades, the god of the Underworld, is said to have loved a nymph called Minthe, but when his queen became jealous of this infatuation, she turned the nymph into the herb we have today.

A less romantic story is that the Greeks wore wreaths of mint on their heads after a night of heavy drinking, believing that the herb could reduce the symptoms of expected hangovers. The Romans are thought to have brought mint plants to Europe, from where the herb was taken to Britain and then to America with the settlers.

COOKING

Mint should always be used as fresh as possible and cooked as little as possible. It gives up its flavour wonderfully in hot liquid and mint tea has to be one of the best herb teas in the world (see page 46). You can also dry it at the end of the season to give a smoky, minty flavour to Greek and Turkish recipes, including kebabs and stuffings for peppers and aubergines/eggplants.

Many people add a stem of fresh mint when they are cooking peas, but the herb adds a lot to most other vegetables and pulses/legumes. Adding finely chopped mint, mixed into butter, to the season's first new potatoes is one of life's great pleasures. The herb plays a big part in many recipes from the Middle East, like my Tabbouleh (see page 60), where a lot of both mint and parsley are chopped finely and added to cooked bulgar wheat with tomatoes, cucumber, good olive oil and lemon juice. It is also perfect with summer fruits like strawberries and the variegated mints look particularly good with desserts. They are weaker growers than plain green mints, but are happy in containers.

GROWING

Mint is a traveller in the garden, always looking for pastures new. The best way to control plants is to grow them in large pots of rich, fertile soil, sunk in the garden. Leave the pots protruding slightly above soil level to try to stop the roots escaping. It is a good idea to divide each mint plant in the autumn because the large creeping roots, called runners, wrap around the outside of the root ball and rot in the wet when they touch the sides of the pot. To stop this happening, remove the mint from the pot, saw it in half and replace with the runners in the middle of the pot.

After a couple of years, despite all this effort, many of the most rampant mints will break away from their pots and cause havoc in the garden. One of my favourite mints, Bowles's mint, which is excellent for tea, for mint sauce and for flavouring desserts, is the most successful escapee. So I will now only grow it in containers. This is successful if you use rich compost, place the container in partial shade, keep the soil moist and apply a liquid feed regularly during the growing season.

Mint can suffer from powdery mildew if it gets dry. Cut it back, fertilize and water well to solve the problem. If you get mint rust, the only answer is to destroy the plant. Mint is unreliable from seed, but it is easy to produce new plants from root cuttings. Pinch out flower buds to encourage young side shoots, which will extend the season and produce healthier plants. To encourage a second batch of healthy leaves, cut each plant back after flowering to 5cm/2in above ground. You will soon have new growth.

If you only have space to grow a few mints, I would suggest Bowles's mint, Moroccan mint for Middle Eastern recipes, spearmint, a variegated mint and basil mint, which is excellent with tomatoes and pasta.

MINT

COURGETTES WITH MINT AND FETA

This is a perfect example of the restaurateur and food writer Antonio Carluccio's philosophy that the minimum number of ingredients leads to the maximum flavour. It's a powerful and delicious combination to serve either as an appetizer or side dish.

4 courgettes/zucchini, thinly sliced lengthways
about 2 tsp cooking salt
2 tbsp olive oil, plus extra to drizzle
85g/3oz Greek feta cheese, crumbled
1 small handful of mint, leaves picked and
  chopped
freshly ground black pepper

Put the courgettes/zucchini in a colander and sprinkle with salt, a large pinch to each courgette/zucchini slice. Leave to drain while you heat a griddle pan or barbecue. Rinse the courgettes/zucchini and pat dry. Brush them on both sides with a little of the oil. Cook in batches on the griddle for about 5 minutes until they start to become lined with black. Turn them over and cook on the other side for a further 5 minutes until tender and lined with black. Arrange on a plate, sprinkle with the crumbled feta and mint leaves, then drizzle over a little olive oil. Season with pepper to taste.

Serves 4

Preparation: 15 mins
Cooking: 20 mins

MUSHROOM AND MINT PÂTÉ

This simple pâté can be used as a canapé in small pastry cases or can be served as an appetizer with slices of fresh crusty bread. It is equally successful made with lovage in the place of the mint.

3 large field mushrooms
2 large garlic cloves
2 tbsp olive oil
1 slice of wholemeal/wholegrain bread, made into
  breadcrumbs
30–40 mint leaves, plus extra small leaves
  to sprinkle
310g/11oz/heaped 1⅓ cups cream cheese
sea salt and freshly ground black pepper

Preheat the oven to 180°C/350°F/Gas 4. Put the mushrooms and garlic in a baking dish and drizzle over the oil. Bake for 20 minutes until the mushrooms are tender and the garlic softened. Remove from the oven and leave to cool. Once cool, blend the mushrooms and garlic with the remaining ingredients to a smooth pâté, seasoning with salt and pepper to taste. Serve sprinkled with small mint leaves.

Serves 4

Preparation: 15 mins
Cooking: 20 mins

MINT

TABBOULEH

This is great party dish because it looks glamorous scattered with herbs, vegetables or edible flowers. The traditional Lebanese bulgar wheat gives an earthy quality, balanced by refreshing mint and lemon. When my different coloured Heritage tomatoes are at their best, I use tabbouleh as the base for a tomato treat, with raw and cooked tomatoes, often stuffed with herbs.

115g/4oz/⅔ cup bulgar wheat
6 spring onions/scallions, chopped
1kg/2lb 4oz tomatoes, skinned, deseeded and
    chopped (see page 24), about 400g/14oz
    prepared weight
a large pinch of allspice
4 tbsp chopped parsley leaves
6 tbsp finely chopped mint leaves
90–120ml/3–4fl oz/⅓–½ cup olive oil
4 tbsp lemon juice
2 handfuls of edible flowers, such as marigold,
    thyme, marjoram, dandelion, bergamot, borage,
    heartsease or nasturtium, washed
sea salt and freshly ground black pepper
cooked vine leaves or raw lettuce leaves, to serve

Soak the bulgar in a large bowl of water for 30 minutes – it expands a lot. Drain and squeeze out the water with your hands, then spread out to dry on a dish towel.

When ready, mix in all the ingredients very well and scatter with the edible flowers. Season with salt and pepper. The tabbouleh can be served with whole lettuce leaves or cooked vine leaves, which can be used to scoop up the tabbouleh.

Serves 4

Preparation: 20 mins, plus soaking

BLACK PUDDING WITH MINT AND BROAD BEANS

I like to serve black pudding made by our local butcher, not with a traditional British breakfast of bacon and eggs but with fruit or vegetables, which lighten the strong taste. One of my favourite appetizers is to fry sliced black pudding, shallots and dessert apples with chopped thyme in a knob of butter.

Many countries eat blood sausage, called *morcilla* in Spain, *boudin noir* in France, *mutura* in Kenya and *blutwurst* in Germany, for example. This recipe uses black pudding with young broad/fava beans and mint.

2 tbsp olive oil
250g/9oz black pudding cut into 1cm/½in slices
1 garlic clove, finely chopped
80ml/2½fl oz/⅓ cup vegetable stock
450g/1lb/3½ cups shelled broad/fava beans
1 small handful of mint, preferably spearmint or
    Moroccan mint, leaves picked and chopped
sea salt and freshly ground black pepper
crusty bread, to serve

Heat the oil in a frying pan over a medium heat and fry the black pudding for 2–3 minutes on each side until it darkens. Remove from the pan and keep warm. Add the garlic and fry for a few minutes until it softens. Add the stock and broad/fava beans and cook for up to 5 minutes until the beans are tender. Return the black pudding to the pan and heat through, then add the mint and seasoning. Stir, then serve with slices of crusty bread.

Serves 4

Preparation: 30 mins
Cooking: 15 mins

MINTY CHOCOLATE MOUSSE WITH CRYSTALLIZED MINT LEAVES

Rich and dark – and sinful if you are on a health kick or trying to lose weight! This old favourite is made a little different by adding mint, and will taste very special if you use good-quality dark chocolate with a high percentage of cocoa solids. Apple or Bowles's mint is perfect for this recipe, if you have it, but ordinary mint will work fine. Ideally, make the crystallized mint leaves the day before, so that you can leave them to dry overnight.

250g/9oz dark/semisweet
  chocolate, at least 70% cocoa
  solids, broken into pieces
1 tbsp butter
1 handful of mint
4 eggs, separated

CRYSTALLIZED MINT LEAVES
1 egg white
8 mint leaves
1 tbsp caster/superfine sugar

First make the crystallized mint leaves. Line a flat plate with baking parchment. Whisk the egg white until light and fluffy. Brush it onto the leaves on both sides, then sprinkle with sugar. Lay the leaves on the prepared plate and leave in a warm place to dry, preferably overnight.

To make the mousse, put the chocolate, butter and 150ml/5fl oz/scant ⅔ cup water in a saucepan over a very low heat and melt, stirring all the time, until smooth. Add the mint and submerge in the liquid. Leave to cool, then remove the mint, which will have flavoured the chocolate. Whisk the egg yolks, then whisk them into the chocolate mixture.

In a clean bowl, whisk the egg whites for about 5 minutes until thick and silky. Fold a couple of spoonfuls into the chocolate mixture to loosen it, then gently fold the remaining egg whites into the chocolate until just blended. Turn into individual ramekins/custard cups and leave to set. To serve, top with the crystallized mint leaves.

*Preparation: 15 mins, plus crystallizing,
  cooling and setting
Cooking: 5 mins*

Serves 4

OREGANO AND MARJORAM

Oregano and marjoram are in the same genus and share a warm, spicy flavour. But they are different species and oregano is far more pungent and gutsy, while marjoram is milder and sweeter in flavour. It is ideal to grow both in the garden, using marjoram raw or briefly cooked in subtle recipes, leaving oregano to make its mark on strongly flavoured dishes. The taste of oregano varies according to the climate, having a more intense flavour in hot, dry locations. This has led to its importance in both South American and Mediterranean cooking.

HISTORY

Both of these herbs originated in the Mediterranean before moving on to the rest of the world. Oregano comes from the Greek words *oros* meaning mountain and *ganos* meaning joy. In Ancient Greece it was planted on graves to send the dead happily on their final journey. It was said to be created by the goddess of love, Aphrodite, to bring happiness. So it was woven into crowns to be worn by couples during their wedding ceremonies.

COOKING

Marjoram has a delicate flavour that is easily lost in cooking, so add it at the last moment or use it raw. Its leaves and flowers are wonderful in a green salad, and I use it with many vegetables, including artichokes, courgettes/zucchini and cauliflower. Try it with young, subtle cheeses and in sauces with fish or chicken.

Oregano is far, far stronger. It is one of the few herbs that dries really well and tastes even better dry than fresh in most recipes. I pick the herb just before flowering, when the leaves have maximum flavour, and hang it in an airy place. Once it is dry, I store it in an airtight container where the flavour will last for a few months. Drying brings out its peppery, spicy taste which is crucial for Italian favourites like pizza and tomato sauces. It is used in many South American and Spanish dishes as well as Greek slow-cooked lamb recipes such as Lamb Kleftiko (see page 180), moussaka, kebab marinades and Greek salads. Greek oregano is a particularly intense, even pungent plant, which I grow but use sparingly. I use more common oregano than other varieties, including in my tapenade recipe on page 68. I push it under the skin when I roast chicken, use it to flavour many canapé recipes (see pages 224–5) and add to baked mushrooms and aubergines/eggplants.

GROWING

There are many oregano varieties which are worth growing in the herb garden – including golden, white and variegated – which are all very attractive. I also grow pot marjoram in large clumps in my herb garden and other areas, because I am told by bee experts that it attracts the insects more successfully when it is in flower than any other plant.

I start to get busy with oregano and marjoram in the spring, dividing the large clumps of pot marjoram in my four formal herb beds, sowing seed for Greek oregano in the greenhouse and generally tidying up the different species I grow in well-drained, sunny spots. This year, several plants of pot marjoram were given to the local village school to attract bees and butterflies to their wildlife garden.

I have so many marjoram plants that I do not need to keep cutting them all back to grow fresh leaves. Many are left until very late summer so that bees can enjoy their flowers before I harvest them, dry the big bunches and put the dried leaves and flowers in pot pourri. Dried marjoram, unlike dried oregano, is not good in food, so I always use fresh leaves in recipes. Before the winter, I make sure that all stems are cut right down to the ground.

Oregano and marjoram look good when they are grown in containers. If you visit the British Library in London, have a look at their large pots in the courtyard, which have pot marjoram in the middle with alpine strawberries planted all around the edges. The result is quite unusual but certainly very dramatic. These are plants which thrive in window boxes or pots, so anyone living in towns or cities has the chance to enjoy home-grown, tasty oregano and marjoram in their cooking.

OREGANO AND MARJORAM

BEETROOT BAKED WITH OREGANO, GARLIC AND GOATS' CHEESE

This makes a good first course or a summer lunch when beetroots/beets are small and juicy. For lunch, you can serve it with salami slices and soda bread, or it is also good served with ricotta instead of adding goats' cheese. Use small, fresh, raw beetroot/beets of a similar size, so they cook evenly.

20 small beetroot/beets
75ml/2½fl oz/5 tbsp olive oil
8 whole, unpeeled garlic cloves
2 tbsp chopped oregano
3 tbsp balsamic vinegar
2 rounds of goats' cheese, about
   100g/3½oz each, quartered
sea salt and freshly ground
   black pepper
slices of salami, to serve
   (optional)

Preheat the oven to 190°C/375°F/Gas 5. Leave the skins on the beetroot/beets but wash them well and remove all but 2.5cm/1in of the stalks and all the leaves. Leave the roots intact at this stage. (You can use any young leaves you have removed in salads.) Drizzle them with 1 tablespoon of the oil and wrap in a parcel of foil. Cook in the preheated oven for about 30 minutes until the skins rub away easily.

Remove the beetroot/beets from the foil, removing the skins as you go, and put them in an ovenproof dish with the remaining oil, the garlic, chopped oregano and balsamic vinegar. Season with salt and pepper and mix well. Return to the oven to bake for 15 minutes.

Remove the dish from the oven, turn the beetroot/beet over again in the juices and add the goats' cheese quarters. Cook for another 10 minutes or so until the beetroot/beet is soft to the point of a knife. Serve with slices of salami, if you like.

Serves 4

Preparation: 35 mins
Cooking: 55 mins

PORK LOIN WITH OREGANO TAPENADE AND TOMATO SAUCE

1lb/450g pork tenderloin
1 tbsp olive oil
green vegetables, to serve

TAPENADE
115g/4oz/heaped 1 cup
    pitted olives
1 shallot, chopped
1 garlic clove, chopped
2 tbsp capers, drained and
    rinsed
1 handful of oregano, leaves
    picked and chopped
1 tbsp Dijon mustard
grated zest and juice of ½ lemon
90ml/3fl oz/6 tbsp olive oil
sea salt and freshly ground
    black pepper

TOMATO SAUCE
1 small onion, chopped
1 tbsp olive oil
1 garlic clove, chopped
500g/1lb 2oz tomatoes,
    skinned, deseeded and
    chopped (see page 24), about
    200g/7oz prepared weight
250ml/9fl oz/generous 1 cup
    vegetable stock
1 tbsp finely chopped oregano

This recipe can be made at any time of the year, but it is particularly good when local tomatoes are in season as they will be full of flavour and produce a tasty, herby sauce to go with the pork. This is a very quick and easy recipe to make once you have your tapenade and tomato sauce. I make lots of tapenade when my oregano is at its best and it stores for a week in the refrigerator but can also be kept in the freezer. I also make a lot of tomato sauce to store in the same way when I have a glut of tomatoes. The tapenade can be made with black or green olives, but this dish looks dramatic with the pork coated in either colour, surrounded by the red tomato sauce.

To make the tapenade, put all the ingredients except the oil in a food processor or blender and process until mixed. Season with salt and pepper. With the motor running, gradually add the oil until blended and thickened.

To make the tomato sauce, fry the onion in the oil in a saucepan for about 10 minutes until softened. Add the garlic and continue to fry for a few minutes. Add the tomatoes, stock and oregano, bring to a simmer and cook for about 10 minutes until thick. Season with salt and pepper.

Cut the pork into 12 medallions and beat them out with a steak hammer or a rolling pin to make them thinner. Spread one side of each medallion thinly with tapenade. Heat the oil in a large frying pan. Add the medallions, tapenade-side up, and cook for 2–3 minutes, then turn them over and fry for 2 minutes on the other side. Spoon the tomato sauce onto serving plates and top with 3 medallions per plate. It can look attractive if a crisp green vegetable is served in the middle of each plate with the medallions arranged around it.

Serves 4

Preparation: 40 mins
Cooking: 30 mins

TAPENADE WITH ROAST CHICKEN

This delicious dish takes only minutes to prepare before popping your chicken in the oven to roast, but the addition of tapenade and lemon makes such a difference to the finished result.

1 recipe quantity Tapenade (see opposite)
1 large chicken
12 new potatoes
16 whole olives, pitted
8 lemon quarters
8 whole garlic cloves
a handful of chopped oregano or marjoram
200ml/7fl oz/scant 1 cup dry white wine
sea salt and freshly ground black pepper

Preheat the oven to 190°C/375°F/Gas 5.

Push the tapenade under the skin of the chicken. Put the potatoes, olives, lemons, garlic and oregano in a large roasting pan, then pour over the wine. Sit the chicken on top and roast for about 1½ hours until the bird is cooked through and tender and the juices run clear. Serve with a favourite green vegetable.

Serves 4–6

Preparation: 10 mins
Cooking: 1½ hrs

TAPENADE WITH BAKED AUBERGINES

Tapenade goes beautifully with aubergines/eggplants, and this recipe makes a delicious lunch.

2 aubergines/eggplants
a drizzle of extra virgin olive oil
1 recipe quantity Tapenade (see opposite)
sea salt and freshly ground black pepper

Preheat the oven to 200°C/400°F/Gas 6.

Cut the aubergines/eggplants in half lengthways and score the surfaces with a sharp knife to make a criss-cross pattern. Put them, skin-side-down on a baking pan and drizzle with a little oil. Bake for 20 minutes.

Remove from the oven and spread the tapenade on the cut sides, then return them to the oven for a further 10 minutes until tender and slightly browned.

Serves 4–6

Preparation: 10 mins
Cooking: 30 mins

[WHY NOT TRY...]

+ Tapenade with mini pizzas (see canapé recipes on pages 224–5)
+ Adding 55g/2oz anchovy fillets to the recipe opposite to make a more gutsy tapenade
+ Making tomato tapenade by adding 55g/2oz chopped sundried tomatoes to the tapenade recipe opposite
+ Grilling/broiling some lamb cutlets until almost cooked, then smearing with tapenade and grilling/broiling until cooked to your liking

OREGANO AND MARJORAM

COD WITH OREGANO-BRAISED BROAD BEANS AND A SPICY SALSA

100ml/3½fl oz/scant ½ cup
  olive oil
1 onion, finely sliced
1 garlic clove, finely chopped
450g/1lb/3½ cups shelled
  broad/fava beans
2 tbsp chopped fresh oregano
  leaves or 1 tbsp dried
juice of 1 lemon
4 cod fillets, about 140g/5oz
  each
sea salt and freshly ground
  black pepper

SPICY SALSA
250g/9oz tomatoes, skinned,
  deseeded and finely chopped
  (see page 24), about
  100g/3½oz prepared weight
1 garlic clove, finely chopped
1 red chilli, deseeded and
  chopped
1 tsp sherry vinegar
2 tbsp olive oil

I always harvest and dry lots of oregano, then I use it throughout the year for recipes where the dried herb is better than fresh leaves. For example, it is usually preferred by Italian cooks for their many tomato-based pizza and pasta recipes. During a recent holiday in Sicily in late spring, the food markets were selling bunches of dried oregano, but I did not see fresh leaves for sale. Many Greek and Spanish recipes can use dried or fresh oregano, including this Spanish-influenced fish dish.

Heat about half the oil in a frying pan over a gentle heat and fry the onion for about 10 minutes until softened, then add the garlic and fry for 2 minutes. Add the beans and oregano, then add the lemon juice and pour over enough water to just cover the beans. Season with salt and pepper. Bring to the boil, then simmer gently for 15 minutes until the beans are tender.

Make the salsa by mixing together all the salsa ingredients.

Heat the remaining oil in a frying pan over a medium heat and fry the cod for 4 minutes on each side. Divide the beans among serving plates, top with a piece of cod and serve with the salsa.

Serves 4

Preparation: 20 mins
Cooking: 35 mins

TARRAGON

French tarragon is such a big seller in both garden centres and food shops that it is often described as the "queen of anise-scented herbs". But although I always grow this perennial and use it regularly, I believe it cannot compete with the anise-flavoured annual herb chervil, which can be grown throughout the year, has beautiful leaves and a wonderful taste. But I would not be without tarragon because it has a refined taste which does not overpower food. And it is important for classics, like Bearnaise Sauce (see page 191), tarragon vinegar (see page 147) and omelette *fines herbes* (see page 32).

HISTORY

Tarragon is native to southern Europe, but its use soon spread around the world, including Asia and North America. It is said that the ancient kings of India had a favourite drink made from tarragon and fennel. It was a favourite, too, with Catherine of Aragon, when tarragon arrived in English gardens during her husband Henry VIII's reign. The king is rumoured to have decided to divorce his Queen because of her "reckless use" of this queen of anise herbs.

COOKING

It is important to buy or grow French tarragon. Some people confuse it with Russian tarragon, which has a very inferior flavour.

The anise taste has a natural affinity with chicken, fish, seafood, eggs, mayonnaise, potatoes, cheese, mustard, green beans, salads and tomatoes. It is traditionally combined with parsley, chervil and chives to make *fines herbes*. Tarragon is also successful in sweet dishes with fruits like nectarines and strawberries.

Always use it raw or lightly cooked and treat it with respect. Taste it as you gradually add it to a dish, because its flavour varies greatly in intensity through the season. Use the leaves from early spring until autumn. It has its sweetest aniseed taste in spring, so this is the ideal time to make tarragon vinegar and mustard (see page 147). By the summer the flavour has become more intense and sometimes bitter, so use it carefully because a little goes a long way.

Tarragon does not dry well, so I chop it finely at this time of the year and freeze it in ice cube trays to use during the winter.

GROWING

Tarragon is a half-hardy perennial with long, narrow, dark green leaves, which can grow up to 1m/39in tall. It thrives in well-drained soil in sun or shade and can be successfully grown in pots, or dug out and transferred to pots in late summer, which can then be brought inside in winter. Put tarragon into a pot with plenty of space for the root runners it will produce. Water in the day, never in the evening because it hates to have wet roots. Do not feed tarragon too much as this encourages it to produce fleshy leaves with less flavour. During the winter when the plant is dormant, it is important to keep its soil dry. New leaves will appear far earlier than they would if the tarragon had been left to hide underground in the cold, winter garden.

French tarragon rarely produces seed, but propagates itself from underground runners. These can be used to increase your number of plants. It is easy to do in the spring by digging up an established plant and then easing the roots apart to find white shoots. Break off some roots with these white shoots attached and replant in pots with slightly moist compost. You will soon have new plants. It is important to do this every three years because old plants lose the flavour in their leaves. You can also propagate tarragon in the summer by taking softwood cuttings of the growing tips.

Tarragon can suffer from rust, so if you are buying a plant, look for the signs of this disease, which are small spots of a rusty colour on the underside of the leaves. If you have a plant which develops rust you can sometimes save it. Dig it up, remove and burn all the leaves and wash the rest of the plant, including the roots, so they have no soil attached. Put into a new pot with fresh compost. If this does not work, repeat the process but wash the plant with hot water for a few minutes before replanting.

TARRAGON

TANGY TARRAGON CHICKEN

Tarragon is a classic herb to cook with chicken and this recipe adds extra oomph by using tarragon mustard. As tarragon leaves are at their sweetest in spring, I usually pick a lot of them at this time and make tarragon vinegar as well as tarragon mustard to use for the rest of the year. The mustard keeps well in the fridge and is useful for this recipe and many more.

1 tbsp clear honey
1 large roasting chicken, about 1.8kg/4lb
grated zest and juice of 1 orange, shells reserved
1 small handful of tarragon
150ml/5fl oz/scant ⅔ cup chicken stock
2 tbsp dry sherry
sea salt and freshly ground black pepperr

TARRAGON MUSTARD
2 tbsp Dijon mustard
1 tsp finely chopped tarragon

Preheat the oven to 190°C/375°F/Gas 5. Make the tarragon mustard by mixing together the two ingredients in a bowl.

Combine the tarragon mustard with the honey and spread it over the chicken skin. Put the orange shells and half the tarragon inside the chicken cavity, then season the bird with salt and pepper and put the bird upside down in a roasting pan. Roast the bird upside down for 1½–2 hours, basting regularly with the juices. About 30 minutes before the chicken should be ready, turn it over so that the legs and breasts can brown. Add the orange zest to the juices to soften during the final roasting period. Test that the chicken is cooked by inserting a small, sharp knife into the thickest part of the thigh – the juices should run clear. Remove the chicken from the pan and keep it warm.

Remove the layer of fat from the top of the cooking juices. Add the orange juice, stock and sherry and simmer the juices in the original roasting pan until the sauce is thick and smooth, stirring to deglaze the bottom of the pan and combine everything well. Pull the remaining tarragon leaves off the stems and finely chop them. Stir half into the sauce and simmer for another 2 minutes. Serve sprinkled with the remaining chopped tarragon.

Serves 4

Preparation: 25 mins
Cooking: 2 hrs 10 mins

PRAWNS OF LOVE

Cooking is an act of love, which is why I never serve food to people I do not care for. But serving special food to special friends and family is something I love to do. If you use giant prawns/jumbo shrimp for this dish, arrange two of them head to head and tail to tail, then serve on a heart-shape of red sauce to make this dish look very romantic. I call it the Prawns of Love. You can, of course, make the same recipe using a larger number of smaller prawns/shrimp because they are easier to find in the shops. It will taste the same, but look far less glamorous. You would need 200g/7oz for four people as an appetizer. The aniseed taste of tarragon is perfect with the prawns/shrimp and their rich sauce. In winter, when tarragon has disappeared underground in the garden, the aniseed taste of chervil makes it a good substitute.

2 oranges
8 largest unshelled cooked prawns/jumbo shrimp you can find
1 small red onion, very finely chopped
juice of 2 limes
200g/7oz soft red pimientos from a jar
450g/1lb ripe, red tomatoes, skinned, deseeded and chopped (see page 24), about 200g/7oz prepared weight
1 tbsp chopped tarragon
1 large handful of radicchio, chopped (optional)
sea salt and freshly ground black pepper

Juice 1 orange and cut the other into wedges. Marinate the prawns/shrimp in the orange juice in a non-metallic bowl for 2–3 hours. Marinate the onion in the lime juice for a similar time. Drain, reserving the marinades.

Rub the pimientos and then the tomatoes through a sieve/fine-mesh strainer into a bowl and mix together. Add the chopped tarragon and the fruit juices from the marinades, then season with salt and pepper. Make a heart shape with the red sauce on 4 white plates, arrange 2 huge prawns/shrimp on top of each, also in a heart shape, and add the red onion in the middle of the prawns/shrimp. If you wish, finely chop some radicchio and arrange in a heart shape around the prawns/shrimp and their sauce. Serve with the orange wedges to squeeze over the top.

Serves 4

Preparation: 35 mins, plus marinating

TARRAGON

SCALLOPS IN THE TARRAGON SPRING GARDEN

It is refreshing to serve cooked scallops on a base of tiny spring vegetables, the smallest you can find in your garden or greengrocery. Use a mix of baby vegetables like mangetout/snow peas, carrots, beans, or even young courgettes/zucchini if they are available.

55g/2oz each of 5 baby vegetables such as baby corn, broccoli, carrots, courgette/zucchini and mangetout/snow peas
12 fresh scallops
30g/1oz/2 tbsp butter
1 garlic clove, very finely chopped
2 tsp tarragon vinegar or white wine vinegar
1 tbsp chopped tarragon leaves
sea salt and freshly ground black pepper

Cut the vegetables into strips, unless they are very small, then blanch in boiling water for about 30 seconds, refresh in cold water, then drain, pat dry and arrange on four plates.

Cut the scallops into two pieces. Heat a heavy-based frying pan over a high heat until very hot. Put in half the butter and throw in the scallops. Cook for about 20 seconds, turn over and cook the other sides for the same time. The idea is that the outside of the scallops should be slightly caramelized, but the inside almost raw, just warmed through. Take off the heat and arrange the scallops on the baby vegetables. Put the rest of the butter in the hot pan, add the garlic, then the vinegar and cook for a few minutes until syrupy. Add the tarragon at the last moment, season with salt and pepper and pour over the scallops to serve.

Serves 4

Preparation: 20 mins
Cooking: 5 mins

HERB CHEESES

Cheeses happily take on the flavour of herbs, and the combinations are infinite. These are a few of my favourites, but you can always make your own healthier options from low-fat cream cheese or curd, blended with garlic and chervil, dill or lovage. I put mine in an attractive pot and press a leaf from the herb on the surface.

GOATS' CHEESE FINES HERBES

You can also press chopped herb leaves like thyme or savory into a soft cheese, then leave it for a day.

2 tbsp olive oil
1 garlic clove, crushed
3 tbsp finely chopped tarragon leaves
2 tbsp snipped chives
3 tbsp finely chopped parsley
250g/9oz log of soft goats' cheese
sea salt and freshly ground black pepper
extra tarragon, chives and parsley (*fines herbes*), to serve

Mix the oil, garlic, herbs and seasoning, then marinate the cheese in the herb oil for 2 days, turning from time to time. Drain well, roll in a small amount of extra *fines herbes* and put on the cheese board.

Serves 4
Preparation: 18 mins

SALAD BURNET CHEESE BALLS

Make this recipe in winter when salad burnet, with its mild cucumber taste and attractive, dark green leaves, thrives through frost and snow.

175g/6oz/⅔ cup cream cheese (low-fat, if wished), mashed
85g/3oz Gruyère cheese, grated
a pinch of cayenne pepper
3 tbsp chopped salad burnet leaves, plus extra to finish
sea salt and freshly ground black pepper

Mix the cream cheese with the other ingredients, season and chill for 2–3 hours until firm, then form into small balls and roll in more chopped salad burnet.

Serves 4
Preparation: 22 mins

POTTED STILTON AND THYME

I cannot resist buying a whole Stilton for Christmas and always have plenty left over to make this.

225g/8oz Stilton cheese
55g/2oz/4 tbsp softened butter, plus 150g/5½oz/⅔ cup extra for clarifying
a pinch of ground mace
1 tsp English mustard
1 tsp finely chopped thyme leaves

Mash the cheese with the butter, mace, mustard and thyme until creamy. Pack into attractive pots.

Melt the butter for clarifying over a very low heat. Use a spoon to skim any foam off the top of the butter. Slowly pour the clear butter over the Stilton in the pots, stopping before you reach the milk solids at the bottom of the pan. Leave to set.

Serves 6
Preparation: 15 mins

SUMMER

SUMMER HERBS

Herb enthusiasts look forward to summer because scented, intoxicating flowers join the lush green leaves of the herbs, attracting bees and butterflies and improving the look and taste of food. Summer rain makes it hard for insects, preventing them from flying to the herb garden to collect the nectar they need to survive, so it's a relief when the sun breaks through and I hear the buzz of bees around the sage flowers, chamomile, lemon verbena, geraniums, clove pinks, heartsease, lavender, bergamot, roses and the bees' favourite – pot marjoram. It was the Romans who introduced using flowers in cookery to Britain. The 5th-century cookbook *Apicius* mentions violets, mallow, roses and lavender, all of which I grow and use.

It is a good idea to plant herbs with their flowering times in mind. So I grow thymes which flower early in the summer in the same area as pink, blue and white hyssops and a few types of marjoram, because they all flower later in the season. Borage self-seeds everywhere with its delightful blue or white flowers. When the ground is wet, I move the stray plants, with plenty of soil attached, to areas where I prefer them to grow.

Borage flowers look glamorous in ice cubes and on food. The blue flowers are particularly good on blackcurrant recipes, salads and floating on my Borage and Cucumber Soup (see page 85). Other flowers that are worth growing for the kitchen include the peppery nasturtium, marsh mallow and chives. I also grow scented roses to provide petals for ice cubes, ice creams and sorbets (see pages 110–11), syrups (see page 130) and Rose Petal Jam (see page 104). I use the jam in many ways, but one favourite is the Moroccan speciality, grilled/broiled Quail with Rose Petal Sauce (see page 104).

My herbs and their flowers were useful for my older son's wedding because many of them were used in tussie-mussies for decorating the church pews and marquee. These are posies made from scented herbs and flowers which were carried during the plagues because herbalists believed they were antiseptic, preventing infection as well as disguising smells. I used purple sage leaves and their flowers, rosemary, golden marjoram, lavender, clove pinks, alchemilla and many roses.

At this time of year, it is a good idea to harvest herbs and their flowers for drying, because they are now at their best. Always pick them in the middle of the morning on a warm, dry day when the dew has evaporated. The flowers should be open from their buds but not full-blown. At this stage they have not released too much of their essential oil and will therefore be full of scent when they are dried. Herbs like thyme, mint and oregano are dried in bunches. I hang them over the cooker so that in winter months, when fewer herbs are available, I can give a bunch of lemon thyme, for example, a quick squeeze over a pan, and the leaves will drop into the sauce. Quick and simple. The more delicate herbs like chives, tarragon and dill do not dry well, so they are chopped very finely and frozen with water in ice cube trays.

This is the season when the choice of recipes becomes enormous because all the herbs are thriving. Recently my husband set aside several recipes which he fancied using with the fish he had bought that day. He decided he would choose the recipe based on which herbs were at their best. But when he checked the herb garden, he found that every single one of the recipes was possible because sorrel, dill, fennel, tarragon, chives, parsley, thyme, savory, mint, lovage, chervil, lemon balm and land cress were all in top form in the garden. He chose sorrel, one of his favourites for fish.

Having a well-stocked herb garden means that you never have to rush off to the shops to find ingredients. The best home-grown method of transforming food is there just outside your door and sadly it is hard to find many of my favourite herbs in the shops. Considering the fact that interest in herbs is soaring, it is hard to understand why the range of herbs on sale – and grown in gardens – is so limited. That is why I give away my herbs to local chefs, neighbours and friends.

Late summer is the time to grow salad herbs to supply the kitchen throughout the winter. They do not bolt or become full of holes from flea beetle as they do when I sow them in spring. They also have a better size and flavour. If you are short of space, grow mixed salad herbs, by the kitchen door in a large pot or trough and cut them very young every week to serve as tasty, good-looking salad leaves. As I have plenty of space in my garden, I like to grow different types of cress, mustards, rocket/ arugula and purslane. which I have growing all through the summer months.

[SUMMER ACTION LIST]

+ Thin chamomile seedlings to 15cm/6in apart and make successive sowings of chervil each month.

+ I leave some of chervil's pretty white flowers to set seed, which turn black when they are ready to pick in very early summer. By storing them and sowing regularly, you can have healthy chervil growing for 12 months of the year.

+ Take cuttings of many herbs, including the sage and thyme you are pruning after flowering. Use non-flowering shoots for propagating. Young sage plants in their first year should have the tips of shoots cut back to encourage bushy growth.

+ Thin dill seedlings to 25cm/10in apart. I leave a few flower heads to set seed.

+ Cut lemon verbena and special sages, like blackcurrant, tangerine and pineapple. Use the leaves in summer recipes.

+ Cut off most of the flower heads of lovage as they appear, leaving just one or two to seed. When the leaves start to yellow, I cut them right down to encourage new, green shoots.

+ By mid-summer it is possible to collect the seeds of many herbs. Most of them can be kept for next spring, but angelica seeds must be sown within three months to be viable and lovage seeds should be sown outside in the autumn. Borage seeds always do their own random thing, so I have never collected the seed from this annual herb and sown them in a special area. They always appear the next year and if young plants are found in an unsuitable spot, they are easy to move.

+ Sow annuals like dill, coriander/cilantro and summer savory at the start of each summer month. Basil can be grown outside in summer, too.

BORAGE

Borage is all about its flowers, which are the most exquisite in the herb garden. They are normally blue, sometimes with a hint of pink or purple. But I also grow a white version called Alba. They are delicate, beautifully shaped and coloured, as well as being quite delicious. If you pop one in your mouth, the flower releases a sweet cucumber taste. They make a wonderful addition to drinks, and are often added to Pimm's, perpetuating the joyful combination of alcohol and borage.

HISTORY

Borage is native to the Mediterranean region, and bees love its nectar so much that the herb was once called "bee bread". Throughout history, its flowers have been added to drinks, and the herbalist Gerard said in 1597 that the gallant blue flowers in wine drive "away all sadnesse, dullnesse and melancholy".

COOKING

I scatter borage flowers on salads, summer fruits and soups. The blue flowers look at their best on purple, blue or pink foods – see my recipe for Basil, Borage, Gorgonzola and Figs on page 22. I particularly like using the flowers on a dessert I make with pannacotta, red fruits like strawberries, cherries or raspberries and a blackcurrant coulis. Last spring we took friends for lunch to the Tresanton hotel in Cornwall, UK, where we were surprised to see borage flowers decorating the dessert at that time of year. I asked the chef how he tracked them down, because this herb does not normally flower until summer. He told me they were grown under glass in Essex, far away from Cornwall. Such is their appeal. I also freeze them into ice cubes for celebratory drinks – a classic garnish.

I use the borage leaves for soup (see right), cook them like spinach and chop them up to add to Pimm's, along with fruit, mint and cucumber.

GROWING

Borage flowers, sometimes known as starflowers, appear in early summer and last until the autumn. It self-seeds easily every year and thrives in sunny spots with free-draining soil. Some gardeners grow the herb with vegetables and tomatoes to deter bugs. It will also grow in pots. The leaves are edible but it is wise to pick them young before they become stiff and hairy.

BORAGE AND CUCUMBER SOUP

This is a perfect soup for a hot summer evening and is so simple to make. It looks cool and inviting and your spirits will be lifted by the exquisite blue borage flowers floating on the pale green surface.

2 cucumbers, chopped into 1cm/½in pieces
1 large handful of young borage leaves, picked and chopped
4 spring onions/scallions, chopped
500ml/17fl oz/generous 2 cups chicken or vegetable stock
300g/10½oz/1¼ cups plain yogurt
a pinch of cayenne pepper
sea salt and freshly ground black pepper

TO SERVE
120ml/4fl oz/½ cup double/heavy cream
4 tsp finely snipped chives
16 borage flowers

Put the cucumber, chopped borage leaves and spring onions/scallions in the stock, bring to the boil and simmer for about 5 minutes. Use a stick blender (or transfer to a blender) to blend in the yogurt, then leave to cool and chill until ready to serve.

Season the chilled soup with cayenne, salt and pepper. To serve, swirl a spoonful of cream into each bowl, sprinkle with chives and float the borage flowers on top.

Serves 4

Preparation: 20 mins, plus chilling
Cooking: 10 mins

DILL

Dill has an invigorating, pungent taste, perfect with big flavours like smoked fish, beetroot/beet, mustards and gherkins. It is a delicate-looking, soft herb which is not suited to long cooking and is used most often snipped over prepared dishes, which benefit from its aniseed taste with a hint of citrus. It looks attractive on food and is also thought to stimulate appetite and help digestion. The feathery leaf is not as strongly flavoured as the seed, but both are used in food, as well as whole flower heads, which are added when you are pickling cucumbers or gherkins.

HISTORY

Dill is native to southern Europe and Asia but is now seen growing wild in many parts of the world. The name dill is thought to come from the Anglo-Saxon word *dylle*, which means "to soothe". It was used to calm stomach ache and mixed into gripe water given to babies. More romantically, it was infused in wine to encourage passion. Dill seeds were taken by settlers to North America where it was known as "Meeting House Seed" because children were given it to dull their appetite during long sermons. It is not surprising that in the Bible the Gospel of St Matthew describes using dill as a tax payment because it was so valued.

COOKING

Dill is a popular herb for salmon, so you can usually find it in supermarkets and greengrocers. It will keep for up to a week in the refrigerator. But there is nothing like having it fresh in your garden. Because I let it go to seed to collect for eating and sowing, I can also enjoy the bright yellow flowers, which I pick to cheer up my buttercup-yellow kitchen. As my oldest granddaughter often says: "Yellow is my favourite colour because it is a happy colour."

Dill is one of the most popular culinary herbs in Scandinavia, Iran and Eastern Europe, where it is used with potatoes, pork, fish, eggs, yogurt and pickled cucumbers. The delicate-looking leaves have a deceptively powerful flavour, so you need to be careful with the quantities you use. In most recipes, the herb should be added near the end of the cooking for best results. I like it in pancakes to serve with smoked salmon and it is my favourite herb for lifting the taste of courgette/zucchini soup.

As I do not like the flavour of dried dill, I freeze chopped, fresh leaves in ice cube trays to use during the winter. My recipes on pages 90–1 show how I like it with cucumber and also with pork and gherkin sauce. Dill is good in a mustard sauce for fish, to make smoked salmon and cream cheese pâté, with fresh broad/fava beans, with herrings and in omelettes, rice and many vegetable soups. This herb may look like fennel, but its softer, silkier leaves are more useful in the kitchen.

GROWING

As I like to have dill growing for as long as possible, I make three or four sowings of this annual, starting in early spring. I sow seed directly in a sunny spot, 20cm/8in apart, as it does not like being transplanted. The leaves are ready within two months. The plant normally grows to about 60cm/24in tall, but in some areas grows to 1.5m/5ft.

The small yellow flowers grow in attractive umbels because dill is from the Umbelliferae family of plants. Water dill well so that it does not quickly run to seed and feed with fertilizer. When it eventually goes to seed, harvest the seed heads and leave them to dry completely in a paper bag, then store in an airtight container to use for cooking and also for sowing in the garden the following year. They remain viable for three years if they are stored in a dry place. Dill seed has a warm aniseed flavour and is a traditional pickling spice.

Do not grow dill near fennel as they can cross-pollinate. They share an aniseed taste with other plants like sweet cicely, as well as anise and star anise. This taste comes from an aromatic compound called anethole, which I love in many recipes.

VINE LEAVES STUFFED WITH DILL, PINE NUTS, RICE AND RAISINS

Some of us are lucky enough to have a vine growing in the garden. Others may have a friend who is happy to pass on the leaves, or you can buy preserved leaves from a delicatessen. I like to use them uncooked to decorate a cheeseboard or even a garden table. There are many recipes for stuffed vine leaves, which are often added to a collection of small dishes, or meze, for a first course or light lunch. They are popular throughout the Middle East. Normally minced/ground meat is used to make hot stuffed vine leaves, or dolma. Cold dolma are usually made without meat but with lots of herbs.

250g/9oz vine leaves
2 onions, finely chopped
150ml/5fl oz/scant ⅔ cup
  olive oil
2 garlic cloves, finely chopped
3 tbsp pine nuts
2 tbsp tomato purée/paste
1 tsp ground cinnamon
a large pinch of saffron strands
200g/7oz/heaped 1 cup
  risotto rice
1 tbsp raisins
1 handful of dill, chopped
2 tbsp chopped mint leaves
juice of 2 lemons
sea salt and freshly ground
  black pepper

Soften fresh vine leaves by plunging them in boiling water for a few minutes until they become limp. Preserved vine leaves should be soaked in boiling water for 30 minutes to remove the salt.

Fry the onions in half the oil in a saucepan for about 10 minutes until softened. Add the garlic and continue to fry for a few minutes. Add the pine nuts and fry for about 5 minutes until golden. Stir in the tomato purée/paste, then all the remaining ingredients, except the remaining oil, seasoning with salt and pepper.

Place a vine leaf on a board, vein-side up. Put 1 tablespoon of the mixture at the stem end, fold the leaf over the filling, then fold over both sides towards the middle and roll up like a small cigar. Repeat until you have used all the filling but have a few vine leaves left.

Tear up the remaining leaves and put them on the bottom of a large frying pan to prevent sticking, then pack the rolled up vine leaves tightly in the pan. Pour over the remaining oil and add enough water almost to cover. Simmer gently for 2 hours, topping up with boiling water, if necessary, until the leaves and their contents are soft and juicy. Leave to cool in the pan before serving.

Serves 8

Preparation: 40 mins
Cooking: 2 hrs 30 mins

CUCUMBER PICKLE WITH DILL

This pickle is perfect with many fish dishes. I first made it to serve with fried monkfish tails in a cream and mustard sauce. It cut through and balanced the richness of the dish. For the same reason, it is served in Hungary with rich stews. I also love it with pastrami. The sliced cucumber is salted and pressed to extract the juices, then squeezed and mixed with a delightful sugar, vinegar and dill dressing.

1 cucumber
1 tsp cooking salt
1 tbsp caster/superfine sugar
1 tbsp white wine vinegar
1 tsp chopped dill
freshly ground black pepper

Peel and finely slice the cucumber. Layer it in a colander, sprinkling with the salt as you go, then put a plate and a weight – perhaps a couple of cans – on top and stand it over a bowl. Leave it to press for at least 2 hours. Rinse the cucumber to remove the salt, squeeze it to remove the excess moisture and pat it dry.

In a bowl, mix the sugar, vinegar, dill and pepper, then mix the cucumber with this sweet and sour dressing.

Serves 4

TARTARE SAUCE WITH DILL

It is hard to find good-tasting tartare sauce in a jar. This recipe has a much better flavour and it is quick to make. Well worth 15 minutes of your time. It is perfect with plain fish, it works well with fish cakes and I like to serve it with vegetables. We grow a lot of globe artichokes and I like to separate the hearts and freeze them to use in the winter. My favourite way to serve whole artichokes is to cook them, cool them, then serve them with this tartare sauce for dipping the leaves and eating with the hearts.

150ml/5fl oz/scant ⅔ cup mayonnaise
Dijon mustard, to taste
1 tsp chopped green olives
1 tsp finely chopped gherkins
1 tsp rinsed and chopped capers
2 tsp chopped dill
1 tsp chopped parsley leaves

Mix all the ingredients together and use the sauce to lift many dishes.

Serves 4

Preparation: 20 mins, plus salting

Preparation: 15 mins

PORK WITH GHERKIN AND DILL SAUCE

When I was a student, the meals served in college were dismal and one of my friends there made me feel worse by describing in mouth-watering detail the wonderful recipes her family cooked at home. One dish she raved about was this one, which originated in Eastern Europe. She did not know the exact recipe, but the idea appealed to me so much that I devised my own version and have been eating it regularly ever since.

My older son, who left home many years ago, asked if I could serve this dish over the last Christmas holidays because he missed it so much. Gherkin sauce works with any pork, but I usually use pork steaks or chops. The gherkins are sold in jars with dill, mustard seed and vinegar.

When I have some leftover brown bread, I make it into breadcrumbs in the food processor and put it in plastic bags in the freezer so I always have some available for this and other recipes.

4 pork chops or steaks, about
  140g/5oz each
2 tbsp olive oil
175g/6oz/3½ cups brown
  breadcrumbs or panko
  breadcrumbs
2 garlic cloves, chopped
1 tbsp plain/all-purpose flour
185ml/6fl oz/¾ cup vegetable
  stock
2 gherkins, each about
  13cm/5in (which may be
  sliced into quarters in the jar),
  thinly sliced
1 tbsp chopped dill
sea salt and freshly ground
  black pepper
cabbage and mashed potato,
  to serve

Preparation: 15 mins
Cooking: 20 mins

Brush the pork with half of the oil and season with salt and pepper. Put the breadcrumbs in a shallow bowl and coat the pork with the breadcrumbs. Heat the rest of the oil in a heavy-based frying pan over a medium heat. Add the pork and cook for about 5 minutes on each side until it is golden brown. Leave to rest in a warm oven.

Add the garlic to the pan and fry for 30 seconds, then stir in the flour. Pour in the stock very gradually, stirring continuously, until you have a smooth sauce. I often add a little of the dill vinegar from the pickle jar. Add the gherkins, raise the heat to high and cook vigorously for several minutes until the gherkins have softened and the sauce has thickened. Add the dill, cook through for a minute or so, then serve with the pork and vegetables.

Serves 4

CRAB-FILLED COURGETTE FLOWERS WITH TOMATO AND DILL SAUCE

I grow lots of courgettes/zucchini, and I like to cultivate both green and yellow to make recipes look more interesting. I also make good use of the flowers, stuffing them with several different mixtures, the most simple being cream cheese mixed with a herb such as chives. There is actually a difference between the male and female flowers, and although some chefs – like Ruth Rogers, the founder of the River Café in London, for example – believe the male flowers are superior, I use both. And that's despite a friend telling me I had just said "the most pretentious thing she had ever heard" when I explained that I had recently bought my first-ever deep fat fryer just to cook my courgette/zucchini flowers in batter!

12 small courgettes/zucchini
  with flowers attached
230g/8oz crab meat, ideally
  55g/2oz brown and
  175g/6oz white meat
2 shallots, finely chopped
45g/1½oz/3 tbsp butter
750g/1lb 10oz tomatoes,
  skinned, deseeded and finely
  chopped (see page 24), about
  300g/10½oz prepared weight
4 tbsp dry white wine
4 tbsp fish stock
2 tsp chopped dill
sea salt and freshly ground
  black pepper

Preheat the oven to 190°C/375°F/Gas 5. Remove the stigma from each flower and wash to remove any insects. If the flowers break off while you are preparing the dish, as they tend to, do not worry. Stuff the flowers with the crab meat.

To make the sauce, soften the shallots in the butter over a low heat for about 10 minutes, then add the tomatoes and simmer for 4 minutes. Add the wine and stock and continue to simmer for about 5 minutes until it reaches the consistency of single/light cream. Add the dill and season with salt and pepper to taste.

Arrange the courgettes/zucchini and their flowers in an ovenproof serving dish. Pour over the sauce and cook in the oven for 7 minutes until the baby courgettes/zucchini are tender but still firm.

Serves 4

Preparation: 30 mins
Cooking: 30 mins

EDIBLE FLOWERS

I believe that flowers can taste as good as they look. There are more than 100 edible flowers grown in the UK alone and I have dozens of these in my garden. I welcome the earliest flash of colour in the year from primroses and violets which, like all the flowers I eat, can be scattered on salads, puddings and savoury dishes or incorporated into cooked recipes. It is also worth crystallizing flowers to extend their life for decorating food.

There is nothing new about eating flowers. The Ancient Greeks and Romans enjoyed them and Middle Eastern cooks were thought to be the first to use marigolds in their food centuries ago. John Evelyn wrote about adding flowers to "other salleting" (salads) in the 1600s, and Hannah Glasse recorded recipes that used flowers in the 18th century.

The taste can be powerful, so use them carefully. Herb flowers are a good place to start experimenting, as they normally taste milder than their leaves. Try basil flowers over a tomato and mozzarella salad, delicate cow parsley-like coriander/cilantro blossoms with prawns/shrimp, sage flowers in salads and fennel over fish.

You can now buy nasturtium and pansies, for example, in food shops, but it is better to grow your own if you can. You will know they are chemical free and have not been picked from hedgerows near polluted roads. The best time to harvest flowers is in the morning after any dew has dried but before the heat of mid-day. Herb flowers have their highest oil concentration and flavour just before the blooms are fully open.

Wash them, dry on paper towels and store for a short time in a freezer bag at the bottom of the refrigerator. If you are adding them to a salad, put a dressing only on the salad leaves and add the flowers at the last moment before serving.

Borage is my favourite edible flower because of its true blue beauty, delicate shape and delicious cucumber taste. It was popular with the Ancient Romans and still grows wild in some areas. I find the plants pop up everywhere, even in long grass, so I move young plants when the ground is wet to areas where they will thrive. Borage adds style and taste to desserts, soups, salads and drinks. Like many people, I add them to ice for drinks and I am known by the children in our village as "the woman who puts flowers in her ice cubes". You can also freeze them in olive oil to add later to cold soups. Blue anchusa, rose petals, violas and chive flowers can also be frozen in water or oil.

Primrose and violet plants edge one of my herb beds, bringing subtle colour and flavour to recipes. I use both the flowers and leaves of primrose in salads and their flowers, like violets, can easily be crystallized.

Day lily flowers have a crunchy texture and a peppery taste. They can be added to salads or stuffed with a herb filling before being sautéed.

Pinks or Dianthus have a spicy scent and delicate flavour. I particularly like using the subtle variety called Clove Pink.

Cornflowers have a strong blue colour and spicy-sweet flavour. The petals are sold dried in France but fresh are always better. Stir into egg dishes or pasta sauces and serve in salads.

Viola flowers combine fragrance with subtle flavour and look gorgeous on the plate. All plants in the viola family are suitable but I particularly like the small British native that grows wild in Scotland, *viola tricolour* or Heartsease. It is easy to grow from seed and with luck will self-seed once established.

Pot marigold petals add a hint of pepper and nuttiness to food like soups, risotto, tabbouleh and casseroles, and the bold orange petals make salads and beetroot/beet dishes look special. They also look good against the pale green of chilled vichyssoise or lettuce soup. Try making a cheese soufflé scattered with marigold petals or scrambled eggs with chopped petals added just before the eggs are done. Using the petals is one way of adding colour to rice dishes, so they can be substituted for saffron.

Nasturtiums are widely used in food for their punchy, peppery taste and dazzling colour. Try a dish of cooked prawns/shrimp with lemon juice and sliced avocado, served on a bed of lettuce with salad dressing and nasturtium flowers. As well as salads, try them chopped and mixed into mayonnaise or in fishcakes. Use the flowers shredded in cream cheese or risotto.

More edible flowers include the pale blue chicory or endive, wild garlic, thyme, chervil, bergamot, chives, honeysuckle, dandelion, chamomile, marsh mallow, sweet woodruff, Japanese chrysanthemum, lavender, garlic chives and sweet rocket/arugula. My grand-daughters (see above) help me sow seeds in spring, including nasturtiums and pot marigolds. This may be one reason why they love wandering around the garden picking edible flowers and salad herb leaves for a salad, which they proudly mix and put on the table with a meal. These dishes can only be made at a certain time of the year with home-picked flowers. That is what gives them their magic and makes them memorable.

CRYSTALLIZING FLOWERS
The simplest technique for crystallizing flowers such as rose petals is to dip them in egg white that has been forked through, then sprinkle them with caster/superfine sugar. For more complicated flowers, hold them by the stalk and use a paint brush to coat them with egg white, then sprinkle. Leave them to dry for 24–48 hours on baking parchment. Handle them carefully as they will be brittle. Store in an airtight container for up to a week.

HYSSOP

Hyssop is valuable for its thin, spicy leaves with their hint of lemon, rosemary and mint, while the flowers cheer up the garden in late summer when there's little other colour. I grow the blue, white and pink flowering hyssops, which attract bees and butterflies and offer plenty of edible flowers for salads, egg dishes and puddings. They are near the thyme plants, as they also like sunny conditions and once the faded thyme flowers have been cut back, the hyssops are soon in bloom.

HISTORY

A Mediterranean herb, hyssop has also been cultivated in European gardens for hundreds of years. It was taken to the New World to use in herb tea and tobacco, and was also thought to have antibiotic qualities. It is said that Hippocrates recommended hyssop for chest complaints and lepers were bathed in hyssop water. Hyssop is mentioned in the Bible several times. In Exodus it is explained that the herb is used for putting the blood of sacrifices on doorposts on the night of Passover.

COOKING

Because of its strong flavour, it is used in bouquet garni, stuffings and with game, especially rabbit and venison. But the fresh leaves are also good in syrups to flavour fruit. I like to mix it with lemon, sugar and water to make a syrup that lifts the taste of poached peaches or plums.

GROWING

There are several species but the best known is *Hyssopus officinalis*, which has bright blue flowers. Hyssop is a semi-evergreen hardy perennial, which flowers from summer into the early autumn and grows 1m/39in high. It can also be trimmed back to use as a low hedge. I collect seeds in autumn and sow them inside in early spring, before planting them out 30cm/12in apart. The only exception is rock hyssop, which is a third of the height with dark blue flowers, and can only be propagated by cuttings.

RABBIT WITH PLUMS, PORT AND HYSSOP

Wild animals are normally healthier than farmed animals because their active lives mean they are lower in saturated fat. This is certainly true for wild rabbits, which also have more flavour than the paler-fleshed domestic, farmed rabbits so popular in France.

I eat wild rabbit by choice, but although we have many running around our patch, chopping off the flower heads as they go, I cannot bring myself to kill and cook these resident animals. There has to be a distance between death and dinner. So I buy wild rabbit from our butcher – and ask him to joint it for me – especially when my brother visits. It is his favourite food and I cook it for him with mustard sauce, with lemon and cream or with plums. All these recipes of mine use hyssop, which is especially good with rabbit because its hot, minty flavour counteracts the richness of the wild flesh. The plums I use in this recipe are a local species called Pershore Purple, which we planted in a small orchard 20 years ago. But any plums are suitable for using in this dish.

1.4kg/3lb 2oz wild rabbit, jointed
1 tbsp plain/all-purpose flour
1 tbsp olive oil
1 onion, finely chopped
3 garlic cloves, finely chopped
2 tsp finely chopped hyssop leaves
400g/14oz plums, pitted
100ml/3½fl oz/scant ½ cup port
sea salt and freshly ground black pepper
new or mashed potatoes and a steamed or boiled green vegetable, to serve

Preparation: 25 mins
Cooking: 2 hrs 30 mins

Preheat the oven to 180°C/350°F/Gas 4. Wash the joints and pat them dry on paper towels, then dip the pieces in well-seasoned flour.

Heat the oil in a flameproof casserole dish and fry the rabbit pieces over a medium–high heat for a few minutes until browned, then remove them from the dish and leave to one side. Turn down the heat, add the onion and garlic to the dish and fry for about 10 minutes until softened. Add the hyssop and plums, then put the rabbit pieces on top and pour over the port. Cover the dish with parchment paper and the lid. Cook in the oven for about 2 hours, checking the rabbit after an hour and then every 15 minutes. The flesh should be soft but not falling off the bone.

When it is cooked, take out the rabbit and leave it to rest in a warm place, covered in foil. Meanwhile, boil the juices over a high heat to concentrate the flavour and until the sauce is the consistency of double/heavy cream. Season to taste with salt and pepper. Serve the rabbit and sauce with potatoes and a simple green vegetable.

Serves 4

LAVENDER

No garden should be without lavender, with its sensual combination of beautiful flowers and heady scent. I use it for perfumed hedges, dividing different parts of the garden. It is wonderful to suddenly come across the overwhelming colour of fields of lavender being grown commercially in Provence and other areas. But everyone can enjoy this plant on a small scale because it grows happily in pots.

HISTORY

Lavender is native to the Mediterranean, but now grows around the world. The Ancient Romans enjoyed it in their bathwater and in 1620 the Pilgrim Fathers took the plant with them to America. It has been used for centuries in the UK as an insect repellent and odour suppressor, usually strewn on floors.

COOKING

I dry lavender to mix with rose petals and herb flowers in pot pourri and to scent log fires. It also adds a floral, aromatic flavour to lamb and chicken recipes. I make lavender sugar every summer (see page 132), which I store in jars over winter for cakes and biscuits. Lavender Syrup (see page 130) is made within minutes from flower buds, sugar and water. I use this with strawberries, peaches and raspberries. But I also infuse cream or milk with lavender when I am making desserts, including ice cream, and lavender is used in my Apple and Herb Jelly (see page 166), one of my favourite jellies.

GROWING

Grow varieties of *Lavendula angustifolia* for the best taste. Its common name is English Lavender and I recommend Dwarf Munstead and Hidcot for hedging. Use flowers, buds and even young leaves in food through spring and early summer. You can grow new plants from cuttings, but they rarely "come true" if you try growing from seed. They thrive in sunny, free-draining soil. If you do not have these conditions, add lots of grit when planting.

Cut back in spring and summer. The normal advice is to replace plants when they become leggy, usually after three to five years. But I avoid having to do this by cutting right back into the wood after the summer flowers, after advice from a lavender farmer in the UK. I have not lost a lavender plant yet in the 20 years they have been growing in my garden.

LAVENDER LAMB

The lavender fields in Provence are an inspiring sight, but farmers in other parts of the world are also producing lavender on a large scale, so it is now easier to buy lavender products, like lavender honey and sugar. Many of us grow this wonderful plant in our gardens or in pots on the balcony or veranda. This could be why it is being used more often in recipes, sweet and savoury. Lavender and lemon chicken is a speciality of one of my closest friends and I like to make Lavender Lamb.

1 small leg of lamb, about 2.5kg/5lb 8oz
2 garlic cloves, sliced
2 tbsp lavender flowers, preferably fresh
2 tbsp lavender honey or clear honey
120ml/4fl oz/½ cup dry white wine
90ml/3fl oz/generous ⅓ cup lamb stock
sea salt and freshly ground black pepper

Make holes in the surface of the lamb with the tip of a sharp knife and push in the garlic slices. Crush the lavender flowers in a pestle and mortar, then mix with the honey and season with salt and pepper. Spoon over the lamb and leave for up to 4 hours at room temperature.

Preheat the oven to 220°C/425°F/Gas 7. Put the lamb in a roasting pan and cook for 1 hour, or longer if you do not like the meat pink. Lift the meat out of the pan, cover with foil and leave to rest in a warm place for 15 minutes before carving and serving. While the meat is resting, put the roasting pan with its meat juices over a low heat, add the wine and stock and deglaze by stirring up anything stuck to the bottom. Simmer until you have a sauce of a good consistency, smooth and thick, and serve with the lamb.

Serves 4
Preparation: 15 mins, plus marinating
Cooking: 1 hour 15 mins

ROSE

Roses are the most beautiful of all flowers. I particularly love old roses, for their scent, their form and their colours. June is my favourite month in my garden because the roses are at their best. When the buds first open, the delicate petals and sensuous smells are exhilarating. Every year I am stunned by their perfection. Perhaps my favourite is *Rosa mundi*, with its stripes in different shades of pink, planted centrally in the formal beds of the herb garden.

HISTORY

The earliest roses were grown in Persia, but their fame soon transported them to Greece and then to Rome. Food writers in ancient books produced recipes using scented roses, so they soon became loved for their flavour as well as their looks and fragrance. Pickled rose buds, rose jams, syrups, vinegars and other conserves were popular. Roses have to be heavily, headily fragrant to work in food, so early choices were the Apothecary's Rose, *Rosa gallica*, the Damask Rose and the Rugosa Rose. They all have deep-coloured petals, which make recipes prettily pink. And they are still popular today.

COOKING

To capture the rose fragrance you need lots of petals wilted in hot water. This produces a brown mess, but once the mixture is strained, the magical perfume and flavour of roses remain in the liquid. To make a herb syrup, which is delicious in champagne, cordials, ice cream and summer fruit recipes, follow the instructions for Rose Petal Jam (see page 104), strain the petals and reduce the liquid to the consistency you want.

You can make rose liqueur by filling a jar with a mix of two-thirds petals and one-third sugar and pouring over vodka. Seal, shake and store in a dark place. Shake again regularly and after a few months you can strain the mixture for a rose-flavoured winter treat. Or you can flavour a jar of sugar with a handful of rose petals (see page 132).

For winter rose scent, I dry rose petals for pot pourri, but in Morocco and parts of the Middle East dried rosebuds and petals are ground into a popular spice and rosebuds are often added to meat stews. Dried petals and buds are sold in the markets, as well as rosewater, which is used in many local recipes.

When rose petals are at their summer best, I scatter them over desserts or salad leaves, often with other edible flowers. Add petals when you are poaching fruit like peaches or making fruit salad, or use with pears or quince in an autumn tart. One delicious idea is to mix strawberries or raspberries with pieces of meringue, rose petals and rose syrup. Rose petals can also be crystallized using the method described on page 95.

Do not use shop-bought roses for cooking because they may have been sprayed with chemicals. Pick newly opened roses in the middle of the morning, after the dew has dried but before the important oil has been driven off by the hot sun. Any heavily scented roses, of any colour, are suitable for cooking. Shake the flowers to remove insects, then pull off the petals and remove the bitter white heel on the base of each petal.

GROWING

Grow your roses in well-drained soil in a sunny spot. Enrich the soil with manure or rose fertilizers in spring, after their first flowering, and in late autumn. Then you should never need to spray them with chemicals because they will be healthy enough to resist insect pests and rose diseases. Leave birds, hoverflies and ladybirds to deal with any aphids that dare to pay the roses a visit.

Pests are also reduced by companion planting, using several species. My roses grow through a sea of forget-me-nots and blue nigella, with spires of foxgloves, salvia, Jacob's ladder and exotic opium poppies. Prune roses by early spring, deadhead after the early summer flowers have died and water in dry weather. Then you will have the most beautiful flowers, with perfect petals to flavour exciting food.

QUAIL WITH ROSE PETAL SAUCE

After less than three hours flying from London to Morocco, I was amazed to arrive in a country with a completely different culture, architecture and food. I loved the roses everywhere – in gardens, scattered in baths and fountains – and, of course, in food. Rose Petal Jam is popular in sauces, for rice pudding and in ice cream.

4 boned quail, cut down the middle of the
  backbone with scissors and flattened out
boiled rice, mixed salad and a few fresh rose
  petals, to serve

GARLIC AND ROSEWATER MARINADE
1 garlic clove, crushed
1 tsp ground cumin
½ tsp ground cinnamon
1 tbsp lemon juice
2 tbsp rosewater or 4 tbsp lemon juice
sea salt and freshly ground black pepper

ROSE PETAL SAUCE
4 tbsp Rose Petal Jam (see right, or from a
  delicatessen, Turkish or Indian shop)
½ tsp ground cinnamon
1 tbsp olive oil
1 garlic clove, crushed

Mix together the marinade ingredients and season with salt and pepper, then rub the mix over the quail. Cover and leave in the refrigerator for at least 3 hours or overnight.

Preheat the grill/broiler. Grill/broil the quail for about 5 minutes on each side until browned and cooked through. Test by piercing with a skewer to check that the juices run clear.

Meanwhile, mix together the sauce ingredients in a small saucepan over a low heat, season and warm through, stirring gently. Serve the grilled/broiled quail on a bed of boiled rice with a crisp salad, all scattered with fresh rose petals, and the sauce alongside.

Serves 4

Preparation: 10 mins, plus marinating
Cooking: 10 mins

ROSE PETAL JAM

The Apothecary's Rose, *Rosa gallica officinalis*, *Rosa mundi* and Tuscany Superb are perfect for this recipe, but use any scented roses. The jam keeps for up to 12 months.

400g/14oz rose petals, preferably dark pink or
  red, chopped
400g/14oz/2 cups caster/superfine sugar
juice of 2 lemons
2 tbsp rosewater (optional)

Put the petals in a saucepan with 600ml/20fl oz/ 2½ cups of water, bring to the boil and simmer for about 10 minutes, or until tender. Add the sugar and lemon juice and cook for 10 minutes until the syrup thickens. It should now have a strong rose taste, but if not, add a little rosewater. Pour into warm, sterilized jars (see page 166), cool, then store in a cool, dark place.

Makes about 4 x 400g/14oz jars

Preparation: 20 mins
Cooking: 25 mins

ROSE GARDEN SALAD

Nothing looks more attractive on the plate than this garden salad made with salad herbs, many different edible flowers and fragrant rose petals. All the ingredients are a pleasure to grow, to pick, to arrange in a large dish and then, of course, to eat. Because our granddaughters began helping me grow annual herbs and edible flowers when they were very young, they cannot resist getting involved in making this salad. And they make it a work of art. Serve it as a side salad or a light lunch with bruschetta.

4 large handfuls of mixed garden leaves, such as sorrel, purslane, rocket/arugula, red mustard, mizuna, Greek cress, golden mustard
1 large handful of edible flowers, such as borage, chicory/Belgian endive, violas, pinks, nasturtiums, rocket/arugula flowers and many other herb flowers
1 large handful of deep pink or crimson scented rose petals
juice of 1 lemon
olive oil, for drizzling
sea salt and freshly ground black pepper

BRUSCHETTA (OPTIONAL)
4 slices of good bread, such as sourdough
1 garlic clove

Preparation: 18 mins
Cooking: 10 mins

If you are serving bruschetta, preheat the grill/broiler, then toast the bread on both sides. Rub the garlic clove over one surface of each slice and drizzle with olive oil.

Wash and spin dry the leaves and flowers. Assemble the salad herbs on a large dish, sprinkle over the flowers and then the rose petals on top. Season well with salt and pepper and drizzle with oil and lemon juice.

Serves 4

ROSE CAKE WITH HERB CREAM AND RASPBERRY COULIS

5–6 rose-scented geranium leaves, preferably Attar of Roses variety
4 eggs
175g/6oz/scant 1 cup caster/superfine sugar
250g/9oz/2½ cups ground almonds
butter, for greasing

HERB CREAMS
12g/½oz/1 tbsp gelatine powder
500ml/17fl oz/generous 2 cups double/heavy cream
350g/12oz/scant 1½ cups thick yogurt
3 tbsp herb-infused sugar (see page 132) made with rose geranium leaves

HONEY AND ROSE SYRUP
4 rose geranium leaves, chopped
2 tbsp rosewater
2 tbsp clear honey
juice of 1 lemon

RASPBERRY COULIS
225g/8oz/1⅔ cups raspberries
about 300ml/10½fl oz/1¼ cups stock syrup (see page 130) to just cover the raspberries in a bowl
1 tbsp rosewater
lemon juice to taste (optional)

Preparation: 50 mins, plus chilling
Cooking: 1 hr

This is the favourite dessert recipe that I serve to friends, family or to people coming along to my herb cookery courses – Hann's Herbs. I scatter the pink rose petals on a glamorous plate, sit the marvellous cake on top and sprinkle with geranium flower petals. It is served with individual herb creams made in small fluted moulds. Raspberry coulis finishes the flowery dish. I also make the herb cream for six to eight people in a large antique jelly dish.

To make the herb creams, put the gelatine in a bowl with 5 tablespoons of the cream and leave to soak for about 15 minutes. While it is soaking, put the remaining cream, the yogurt and sugar in a small saucepan over a low heat until the sugar melts. Then add the gelatine mixture to the warm cream and whisk until amalgamated. Rub through a sieve/fine-mesh strainer, then pour into eight fluted moulds about 7cm/3¾in across, and leave at room temperature to set. (Instead of herb sugar you can infuse the yogurt with several rose geranium leaves for a few hours before making this recipe.)

Preheat the oven to 190°C/375°F/Gas 5, grease an 18cm/7in cake pan and arrange the leaves face down on the base. Beat the eggs, then add the sugar and continue to beat until the mixture forms soft peaks when you lift out the whisk. Fold in the ground almonds. Spoon the mixture into the prepared pan and bake for 45 minutes until well risen and slightly springy to the touch.

While the cake is baking, put all the syrup ingredients in a pan with 8 tablespoons of water and simmer until reduced by half. Pour through a sieve/fine-mesh strainer to remove the leaves, then pour the hot syrup gently over the cake. Leave to cool in the pan before turning out. (You can use the same technique with bay and with pineapple or blackcurrant sage.)

To make the coulis, liquidize the raspberries in the syrup, then strain and add the rosewater. Sharpen with lemon juice, if necessary. Serve the cake with the coulis and the herb creams on the side.

Serves 8

HERB ICES

Ice creams and sorbets flavoured with herbs are a cool and wonderful way to end a meal. I have been inspired by the huge range of recipes from the Victorian writer and cook, Mrs Isabella Beeton. I have six coloured drawings of sophisticated food from her books on the walls of my kitchen. And I have several of her old books, including the enormous *Book of Household Management*. She loved recipes for sorbets and ice creams. One book, *Cold Sweets*, published in 1925, has over 60 different iced recipes as well as pictures of ices and drawings of complicated moulds used for freezing the creations.

I have devised many iced recipes over the years but I am particularly delighted with my Bay Ice Cream and Sorrel Ice Cream. Homemade ices have a purity of flavour as they are made from fresh ingredients. I like ice cream smooth and rich, so I use egg yolks, sugar and double/heavy cream, infusing the hot mixture with herbs for flavour.

But making sorbets and ice creams by hand can be hard work and sometimes a bit hit and miss. Unless you want to whisk them with a fork or electric beater from time to time as they freeze, you'll need a machine. The cheap, compact version I have used for over 20 years, is made up of an insulated bowl that needs to be frozen for 24 hours before making the recipe. Or, for ten times the price, you can buy large machines that make an ice cream or sorbet at the touch of a button. One model even plays the ice-cream van jingle to tell you the ice cream is ready!

My recipes using double/heavy cream and egg yolks are not as healthy as making ice cream with thick yogurt, but they are delicious and they work. If you make ice creams with half-fat milk or sorbets with too much water they can turn out solid or crystalline. A machine makes it easier to achieve an ice of perfect consistency and to time it for serving towards the end of the meal. To make ice cream by hand, put the mixture in a plastic tub and remove it from the freezer every few hours, breaking up the ice crystals with a fork. Do this three or four times during freezing.

If you are storing homemade ice cream in the freezer, take it out to soften in the refrigerator about 25 minutes before you plan to serve it.

BASIC ICE CREAM
Starting with a basic ice cream custard, you add favourite herbs for flavour much like you can add a vanilla pod/bean to a recipe. The three I describe here are very special to me. But other herbs like lavender and thyme work well, too. It is worth experimenting.

500ml/17fl oz/generous 2 cups double/heavy cream
5 egg yolks
100g/3½oz/½ cup caster/superfine sugar

Gently heat the cream to just boiling point. Take off the heat immediately and leave to cool.

In a large bowl, beat the yolks and sugar together. Pour the cooled cream into this mixture, beating all the time. Transfer the mixture to a saucepan and heat very gently until the mixture thickens, stirring all the time for at least 10 minutes. Take care not to overheat because you could end up with something looking more like scrambled egg than smooth custard. Cool and store until you want to make the ice cream either with a machine or in the freezer, as described opposite.

Ice creams and sorbets all serve 4–6
Preparation: 10 mins, plus cooling and freezing
Cooking: 20 mins

BAY ICE CREAM

Adding bay lends the ice cream a subtle, clove-scented and spicy flavour – and it can also be used as the base for my Bay-Infused Crème Brulée (see page 182).

1 recipe quantity Basic Ice Cream (see opposite)
5 fresh bay leaves

Heat the cream as in the basic recipe, adding 5 bay leaves to the pan. Allow the cream to cool and leave to infuse for a few hours. Sieve out the leaves and continue with the recipe as described.

ROSE PETAL ICE CREAM

Deep pink flowers are good for flavour.

6 large, scented roses
1 recipe quantity Basic Ice Cream (see opposite)
1–3 tbsp rosewater, if needed

Remove the petals and rinse. Trim off the bitter white part at the base of some rose petals. Put the petals in a pan with the cream and heat as per the basic recipe. Allow the cream to cool and leave to infuse for a few hours. Sieve out the petals and continue with the recipe, adding rosewater for extra flavour, if necessary.

SORREL ICE CREAM

This unusual ice cream has a refreshing, lemony flavour and a bright green colour if blended. Using the citric (or ascorbic) acid stops the normal oxidization that would make the sorrel go brown, so it keeps its green colour.

1 recipe quantity Basic Ice Cream (see opposite)
a handful of sorrel (about 80g/2¾oz)
6g/¼oz/heaped 1 tsp citric acid

Make the custard base and leave to cool. Meanwhile, wash the sorrel, spin it dry, remove the stalks and chop finely. Mix the uncooked sorrel and the citric acid into the cooled custard, blend well in a food processor if you want that bright green colour, then continue with the recipe.

SORBETS

Scenting a sorbet with herbs may sound odd, but it produces an exotic and pure taste that is totally refreshing. Many flavours can be added, including thyme, mint, lavender, sweet cicely, rose petals, pineapple or blackcurrant sage, calamint or the lemon verbena here. You can adapt the basic sorbet base for any herbs you like.

LEMON VERBENA SORBET

This is a great recipe to make when you are pruning your own plant or you are able to beg a branch from a friend.

140g/5oz caster/scant ¾ cup superfine sugar
80 lemon verbena leaves
250ml/9fl oz/generous 1 cup dry white wine
juice of ½ lemon

Dissolve the sugar in 500ml/17fl oz/generous 2 cups of water and boil hard for 8 minutes to make a syrup. Add the lemon verbena leaves and 250ml/9fl oz/generous 1 cup more water and bring slowly to the boil. Take off the heat and add the wine. Cover and cool overnight. Sieve out the leaves, add the lemon juice and make it into a sorbet using a machine or the freezer method (see opposite).

SAVORY

Savory is a bold and tasty herb. And it is very prominent in my garden, providing about 6m/20ft of neat, low hedges of the perennial winter savory around my formal herb beds. I also have areas in the beds for annual summer savoury and clumps of the perennial creeping savory with its attractive white flowers. So savory does dominate both my herb garden and my kitchen.

A young German friend who was staying with us recently wanted a very long and detailed tour of my herb collection because he is about to plant culinary herbs by his home and architectural practice in the countryside near Düsseldorf. He persisted in claiming that he did not know the three savory herbs, until I explained the sort of recipes I used them in and he shouted in excitement: "The bean herb. My mother grows it. So many people grow it in Germany."

In fact, the German word for the herb is *bohenkraut*, which means "bean herb". It is apparently very popular for helping to mitigate the unpopular side-effect of eating too many beans. For the same reason, it is often included in recipes for Jerusalem artichokes to cope with inevitable flatulence.

HISTORY
Savory, or *Satureja*, is a Mediterranean herb in the family Labiatae, which has been used for thousands of years to flavour sauces and vinegars. It has a reputation as an aphrodisiac. The passionate satyrs are said to have lived in fields of savory. They would have a good time in my herb garden!

COOKING
I use summer savory with our favourite vegetables – broad/fava, runner and French beans. It has a smell which is a mix of mint and thyme and dries well for using in *herbes de Provence*. It makes a good herb vinegar (see page 147) and I use it a lot in tomato sauces and salads.

Summer savory has a more delicate taste than winter savory, which is one of the most gutsy herbs I grow. Winter savory has paler, bright green leaves which are tougher and need longer cooking, so it is ideal in stews and for using with a variety of dried beans and lentils. This herb is very popular in Malta where it is added to many recipes, especially lamb, potato and tomato dishes. I like roasting thinly sliced potatoes and onions in olive oil with chopped savory.

It is also used in stuffings and for making sausages and salami. Both winter and summer savory have a good, strong flavour, which is useful for anyone on a salt-free diet. As they are so aromatic, I chop them up for a gutsy salad dressing to accompany a gutsy dish. The small flowers are tasty with salads leaves too.

GROWING
I started with one plant of winter savory, but because it is so easy to produce more plants from soft-wood cuttings, I now have long hedges of the herb, which look good in the herb garden all year round.

I grow the annual summer savory from seed in mid-spring, sowing it in light, well-drained soil in a sunny position. It has square, red stems with whorls of small green leaves and pale lilac or white flowers which attract bees. The square stems show that it is related to the mint family. If you allow it to flower it does affect the flavour and if you fail to cut it back it gets far too leggy, so it is important to cut back the plant early in the summer, to give it time for fresh green leaves to form before winter.

Creeping savory is worth having in the herb garden because the white flowers are very attractive in late summer and it looks good at the front of a border. It grows to about 10cm/4in high and my clumps are now at least 30cm/12in in diameter. But the taste is strong and bitter, so I do not use it in the kitchen.

SAVORY RUNNER BEAN SALAD

Runner beans are one of my favourite vegetables, so I always feel sad when their short season ends. I could eat a plate of them on their own, cooked briefly and served simply with butter and pepper. I also love them as a cold side dish with a garlic and savory dressing, or as here, with a mustard and savory dressing.

2 tbsp Dijon mustard
2 tbsp white wine vinegar
120ml/4fl oz/½ cup sunflower or groundnut oil
1 garlic clove, crushed
1 tsp finely chopped savory leaves
400g/14oz runner beans, finely sliced
sea salt and freshly ground black pepper

To make the dressing, put the mustard, vinegar and 4 tablespoons of warm water in a blender and mix well. With the motor running, gradually add the oil until it thickens to a thin mayonnaise.

Take 4 tablespoons of the mustard dressing and stir in the garlic. (Store the rest of the dressing in the refrigerator for future use.) Pound the savory in a pestle and mortar to bring out the flavour and aroma. Add this to the dressing, then season to taste with salt and pepper.

Cook the beans for 4 minutes in boiling water, then drain and refresh in cold water. Drain well again, then stir in the dressing and serve.

Serves 4

Preparation: 15 mins
Cooking: 5 mins

BUTTER BEAN AND SAVORY CAKES

Savory lifts the flavour of all kinds of bean, dried or fresh. Serve these golden cakes with your favourite fish, meat or vegetables. To use dried beans, soak them overnight, drain, cover with fresh water and cook for about 2 hours before you start.

1 tbsp olive oil, plus extra for frying
1 onion, finely chopped
2 garlic cloves, crushed
zest and juice of 1 lemon
2 tsp finely chopped savory
90ml/3fl oz/6 tbsp dry white wine
2 tsp vegetable stock powder
800g/1lb 12oz canned butter/lima beans, drained
2 eggs, beaten
100g/3½oz/2 cups brown breadcrumbs
sea salt and freshly ground black pepper

Heat the oil in a frying pan over medium heat and soften the onion for 6 minutes. Add the garlic and fry for 2 minutes, then add the lemon zest and savory, stir and fry for 1 minute. Pour in the wine, turn up the heat and bubble until most of the liquid has evaporated. Add the lemon juice, stock powder and 90ml/3fl oz/6 tbsp water. Then add the beans and season generously.

Blitz the beans in a food processor for a short time until mashed, but still with some texture. Divide into 4 portions and shape each one into a patty. Dip the patties first into the beaten egg, then into the breadcrumbs to coat thoroughly. Heat the oil in a frying pan and fry the cakes for 3–4 minutes on each side until golden all over.

Serves 4
Preparation: 20 mins
Cooking: 15 mins

DUCK WITH SAVORY AND ELDERBERRY SAUCE

We have lots of elder in the wilder areas of our garden and always look forward to using the cream flowers for elderflower syrup. We store this syrup to make drinks and to flavour recipes. Other people also pick the flowers from our hedgerows, so we often give them our syrup recipe, too. But the elderberries that form from the flowers are far less popular. I do, however, like their earthy taste and use them in chutney. They are also great for this sauce to serve with duck – either the breasts as here, or a whole roast duck. Savory, with its warm, peppery taste, is the perfect herb in this sauce, as it is excellent with fatty meats. I also make the sauce using blackcurrants instead of elderberries, for lambs' kidneys as well as duck. You can use winter or summer savory in this sauce, but winter savory is stronger, so do not add more than suggested. When I serve lambs' kidneys with the blackcurrant sauce, I cook 12 kidneys for four people.

4 duck breasts
230g/8oz/2⅓ cups elderberries or blackcurrants
150ml/5fl oz/scant ⅔ cup chicken stock or stock made from duck giblets
55g/2oz/heaped ¼ cup sugar, plus extra if needed
1 tbsp redcurrant jelly
1 tbsp very finely chopped summer or winter savory leaves
2 tbsp cooking brandy for the elderberry sauce or Crème de Cassis for the blackcurrant sauce
sea salt and freshly ground black pepper

Preparation: 20 mins
Cooking: 30 mins

To cook the duck breasts, score the fatty skin on the breasts in a criss-cross pattern. Heat a heavy-based frying pan, put the duck breasts, skin-side down, in the pan and dry-fry for 12–15 minutes until the skin is golden brown. Pour off the fat. Season the breasts with salt and pepper, turn them over in the pan and cook for a couple more minutes until they are cooked to your liking. I personally find rare, pink duck can be tough and unpleasant, so I serve mine medium to well done.

Meanwhile, wash the fruit and remove the stalks. Simmer in the stock for 5 minutes, then add the sugar and redcurrant jelly and taste for sweetness, adding a little more, if necessary. Add the savory with the alcohol, season with salt and pepper and simmer until you have a good consistency, smooth and thick. Taste for sweetness again and adjust, if necessary.

Slice the duck breasts and serve them with the sauce.

Serves 4

KIDNEYS WITH SAVORY AND MUSTARD

The strong flavour of kidneys works well with this powerful, aromatic herb. I have always enjoyed lambs' kidneys with mustard, but I also like to grill/broil veal kidneys and serve with a savory and anchovy butter.

10 lambs' kidneys
1 tsp finely chopped savory leaves
2 tbsp oil
1 tbsp cooking brandy
1 tbsp Dijon mustard
3 tbsp half-fat crème fraîche or sour cream
sea salt and freshly ground black pepper
spinach or a green vegetable, to serve

Cut each kidney in half and de-vein. Toss the kidneys in the savory and salt and pepper.

Heat the oil in a large frying pan and fry the kidneys for just under 5 minutes, turning half way through, until they are just starting to turn from pink to brown. Be careful not to go beyond this point when they are at their most tender, otherwise they can toughen up. Add the brandy to the pan. Mix the mustard with the crème fraîche, stir into the mixture in the pan and heat through gently. Serve with a simple green vegetable like spinach.

Serves 4

Preparation: 20 mins
Cooking: 8 mins

PORK, JUNIPER BERRIES AND SAVORY

This recipe is quick and powerful, with the combined strong tastes of crushed juniper berries and savory leaves. It is so good we cannot resist eating this every few weeks.

400g/14oz pork fillet
1 tbsp dried juniper berries
1 tbsp finely chopped savory leaves
1 tbsp olive oil
120ml/4fl oz/½ cup dry sherry
sea salt and freshly ground black pepper
sautéed new potatoes and a crisp green salad,
  to serve

Cut the pork fillet across in thin slices and flatten each piece with a steak hammer. Season with salt and a very little pepper because the herb and juniper berries are already a powerful combination. Crush the juniper berries in a pestle and mortar, add the chopped savory leaves and pound those, too, until it is all well mixed. Spread over one surface of the pork medallions.

Heat the oil in a frying pan over a high heat. Add the pork slices, juniper-side up, and cook for 3 minutes, then turn them over and fry the second side for the same time. Add the sherry to the hot pan and let it sizzle and mix with the herb/juniper flavours, stirring to mix in all the juices. Serve the pork with the pan juices drizzled over the top, with new potatoes and a crisp green salad.

Serves 4

Preparation: 20 mins
Cooking: 10 mins

RED CABBAGE WITH SAVORY AND APPLE

This is another of my favourite dishes, made all the more powerful by adding savory. It can be served hot or cold and keeps in the refrigerator for up to a week. My family enjoys it hot with grilled/broiled meat or game, or with ham baked in cider and orange over the Christmas holidays. It is also excellent served cold a couple of days later with a strong Cheddar cheese or Cornish Yarg and good bread.

1 red cabbage

30g/1oz/2 tbsp butter, plus extra for greasing

1 onion, chopped

2 garlic cloves, finely chopped

2 cooking apples, peeled, cored and sliced

3 tbsp finely chopped savory leaves

grated zest and juice of 1 orange

1 tbsp light soft brown sugar

3 tbsp red wine vinegar

sea salt and freshly ground black pepper

Preheat the oven to 170°C/325°F/Gas 3. Quarter the cabbage, remove any damaged outer leaves, cut out the stalk and core, then shred as finely as possible. Bring a large saucepan of water to the boil, add the cabbage and blanch for 2 minutes until just soft, then drain and refresh in cold water.

Melt the butter in a frying pan and fry the onion for 10 minutes until softened, then add the garlic and fry for 2 minutes. Add the apple slices, cook for another 4 minutes, mix in the chopped savory and orange juice and zest, then turn out on a plate.

Mix together the sugar and vinegar with 3 tablespoons of water and season with salt and pepper.

Spoon half the cabbage into a casserole dish, then half the apple mixture and half the sugar and vinegar mixture, then season with salt and pepper. Add the remaining ingredients, repeating the layers. Cover with thickly buttered parchment paper and put on the lid. Cook for at least 2 hours until tender, checking and stirring from time to time, and adding more water if necessary, until the casserole is rich and thick. Adjust the seasoning with salt and pepper to taste and serve either hot or cold.

Serves 8

Preparation: 20 mins
Cooking: 2 hrs 20 mins

THYME

Thyme is one of the most useful and cheerful plants to have in a garden. I grow it not just in the herb garden, but in the gravel of the courtyard, in dry corners, in Cotswold stone walls and even on the top of staddle stones. It thrives in all these different areas because it likes dry, poor, well-drained sites and a sunny position. And I plant thyme alongside other plants which flower at the same time in early summer, just for its looks alone.

HISTORY

Thyme is now popular in all parts of the world, but it grows particularly well in the Mediterranean region, where you can see it thriving in the wild. The Ancient Greeks used it to make incense for their temples and the Romans, who are thought to have brought it to the UK, used it in room purifiers. Very soon, thyme's antiseptic properties became famous. So the herb was used in posies, called tussie-mussies, made up of several herbs which were carried around by both men and women in the hope of warding off disease. The Romans also appreciated the flavour of thyme, adding it to cheeses and liqueurs. In the Middle East it was used centuries ago to become a vital ingredient in za'atar. Its gutsy taste also guaranteed its place with other herbs in bouquet garni and *herbes de Provence*.

COOKING

It can be difficult to decide which thyme plants to grow for using in the kitchen because there is so much choice from hundreds of different species. But I have ended up with several which are attractive and good in food. My most-used species are common thyme, which has an excellent flavour, and lemon thyme, which is added to many of my recipes from chicken and fish to summery sorbets. I also like the spicy orange thyme, French thyme and some variegated thymes. My tiny caraway thyme, which is only 2.5–5cm/1–2in high, is the best species to rub into beef before cooking. I also buy the Middle Eastern spice blend, za'atar, which combines powdered thyme with memorable hints of savory and oregano.

When I cut back thyme after flowering in June, I tie it into bunches and dry them over the Aga. When I need the flavour of thyme in a sauce, I hold the pan under the dried bunch, squeeze it and the leaves drop conveniently into the sauce. It is the perfect herb for bouquet garni, with bay and parsley, and I also make spicy olive oil using dried chilli, bay and thyme. As thyme is a hard herb, it should be added at the start of the cooking process to allow the depth of flavour to develop. But the softer, young leaves are also good pressed into soft goats' cheese and I use them on tomatoes, sprinkled with black pepper and drizzled with olive oil for slow cooking in the oven.

GROWING

The main problem with thyme is that it can die during a cold, wet winter. I always advise people with heavy, clay soil to plant thyme with lots of grit or to put the plants in pots of lighter, well-draining soil and use fleece to protect them during the coldest months. Thyme can also get leggy and ugly. The best way to avoid this is to cut plants back hard after flowering. But if there is still a problem, thyme can be dug out and replanted in a deeper hole. You can also layer thyme when it becomes woody, weighing down the stem to maximise contact with the soil until it grows more roots, which is an excellent way of producing more plants.

Only a few species can be grown easily from seed, so thyme is best propagated from softwood cuttings, using new growth in spring or summer. I put the cuttings in a mixture of compost and grit, perlite or sand. But I do find my creeping thymes are easier to divide and often produce several new plants from one clump, to grow in gravel or in cracks in the paths.

Common thyme at 30cm/12in tall is ideal to keep clipped for edging beds. I grow most of my thymes at the front of my formal beds mixed with blue, pink and white hyssop. This is because when the thyme has finished flowering, the hyssop is just coming into bloom, which guarantees lots of colour in the garden.

THYME

STUFFED THYME AND CHEESE MUSHROOMS

It is always exciting to come across field mushrooms and fungi growing wild. Our 25th wedding anniversary party benefitted from a huge collection of them, because the restaurateur Antonio Carluccio was one of our guests. Known as the "Mushroom Man", he is a fungi expert and explored our neighbourhood, bringing back dozens of varieties. He then cooked them in his magical way. But this recipe is one of my own favourite ways to use field mushrooms. It makes a first course with a powerful flavour, using one large field mushroom per person, served with salad and good wholemeal or soda bread. Cheddar cheese is traditional, but I sometimes use Gruyère or Parmesan. Two mushrooms for each guest makes a filling lunch.

4 large field mushrooms
1 large shallot, chopped
2 tbsp olive oil
1 garlic clove, finely chopped
4 tbsp brown breadcrumbs
2 tbsp finely chopped thyme
  leaves
1 egg, beaten
sea salt and freshly ground
  black pepper

CHEESE SAUCE
55g/2oz/4 tbsp butter
55g/2oz/scant ½ cup plain/
  all-purpose white flour
300ml/10½fl oz/1¼ cups milk
¼ tsp Dijon mustard
115g/4oz mature/sharp
  Cheddar cheese, grated,
  plus extra to sprinkle

Preparation: 20 mins
Cooking: 40 mins

Preheat the oven to 220°C/425°F/Gas 7. Peel the skin away from the mushrooms, remove the stalks and chop them finely. Put the mushroom caps, gill-side up, in an ovenproof dish.

Fry the shallots in the oil in a frying pan over a medium heat for about 10 minutes until soft, then add and soften the garlic. Mix in the mushroom stalks, breadcrumbs and thyme and season with salt and pepper. Take off the heat and leave to cool slightly, then bind the mixture with the beaten egg, and divide it equally over the mushrooms.

To make the cheese sauce, melt the butter in a small saucepan, stir in the flour and cook, stirring continuously, for 2 minutes to cook out the flour and make a roux. Meanwhile, bring the milk to the boil in a separate pan, then whisk in the roux and cook, stirring, until the sauce thickens. Stir in the mustard and the grated cheese and season with salt and pepper. Pour the cheese sauce over the mushrooms and sprinkle the tops with more cheese. Bake for 20 minutes until piping hot and golden on top.

Serves 4

SLOW-ROASTED CHICKEN WITH LEMON AND THYME

Decades ago, I first came across the brilliant combination of an Aga and a chicken brick in a small farmhouse we rented for a holiday. While my London-based young sons loved helping the farmers next door and my husband tracked down home-grown vegetables on sale nearby, I happily tried cooking the slow way. I left a chicken stuffed with lemon and herbs in the brick at the bottom of the Aga all day while we went swimming. Dinner was tender and tasty. So back in London I bought my own chicken brick, which I still use. Wrap a chicken in lots of foil and cook it at a low temperature to get the same result.

1 small handful of lemon thyme
2 lemons
1 large roasting chicken, about 1.8kg/4lb
150ml/5fl oz/scant ⅔ cup white wine
2 tbsp plain/all-purpose flour
120ml/4fl oz/½ cup chicken stock
4 tbsp double/heavy cream
sea salt and freshly ground black pepper
potatoes and a green vegetable or crisp salad leaves, to serve

Preheat the oven to 180°C/350°F/Gas 4 if you want to cook the chicken in 2 hours, or to 160°C/315°F/Gas 3, if, like me, you want to leave it in a very low oven for half a day or more. I use the bottom oven of my Aga.

Chop 1 teaspoon of thyme leaves to add to the sauce. Juice the lemons, then put the remaining thyme and the lemon shells inside the chicken, season with salt and pepper and put it in the chicken brick with the wine.

Cook the chicken for 2 hours in a medium oven or 4 hours in a low oven. Take the chicken brick out and test that the chicken is cooked by inserting a small, sharp knife into the thickest part of the thigh. If the juices run clear, it is ready. Keep it warm while you make the sauce.

Pour the fat off the juices, then pour the juices into a saucepan. Stir in the flour, whisk in the stock, chopped fresh thyme leaves and lemon juice and cook on the hob over a medium-high heat. Stir well until everything is combined, then add the cream and season with salt and pepper to taste. It should taste strongly of thyme and lemon. Serve with potatoes and a green vegetable or crisp salad.

Preparation: 20 mins
Cooking: 2–4 hrs

Serves 4

IT'S THYME FOR BEANS

I love beans so much that I have several jars of dried beans of different types in the larder, ready for soaking overnight, as well as cans of most beans on standby to make a quick lunch. For this dish, you can use whatever kind of beans take your fancy – cannellini, borlotti, black beans or your own particular favourite.

4 tbsp olive oil
1 large red onion, chopped
200g/7oz cooking chorizo, cut into small cubes (optional)
2 x 400g/14oz cans of beans, drained and rinsed
400g/14oz can of chopped/crushed tomatoes
2 garlic cloves, finely chopped
1 large red chilli, deseeded and chopped
1 tsp smoked paprika
2 tbsp chopped thyme leaves
sea salt and freshly ground black pepper

THYME AND LIME SALAD
juice of 2 limes
1 tbsp olive oil
1 tsp chopped thyme leaves
4 large handfuls of crisp, green salad leaves
1 red onion, very thinly sliced

Preparation: 15 mins
Cooking: 25 mins

Heat the oil in a large saucepan and cook the onion and chorizo, if using, for about 5 minutes until the onion is soft and the chorizo has released some of its juices. Add the remaining ingredients and cook for a further 5 minutes. Add enough water just to cover the beans, bring to the boil, then cook for 15 minutes, adding more boiling water if the beans seem to be drying out. You want to serve them in a flavourful sauce. Season well with salt and pepper.

Meanwhile, to make the salad, mix together the lime juice and oil, then add the thyme and some seasoning. Toss the salad leaves in the dressing, then cover with the onion slices. Serve the beans with the thyme and lime salad.

Serves 4

THYME SHORTBREAD

Thyme adds character to this simple shortbread. Use lemon thyme if you have some. This recipe can also be made with young, finely chopped rosemary leaves or fresh lavender flower buds. I like to serve the shortbread with pannacotta and Raspberry Coulis (see page 109).

55g/2oz/heaped ¼ cup caster/superfine sugar
2 tsp finely chopped thyme leaves
115g/4oz/½ cup butter, softened, plus extra for
  greasing
finely grated zest of 2 lemons
175g/6oz/1¼ cups plain/all-purpose flour, plus
  extra for dusting

THYME TOPPING
2 tbsp caster/superfine sugar
1 tsp finely chopped thyme leaves

Preheat the oven to 150°C/300°F/Gas 2 and grease a baking sheet. Beat the sugar, thyme, butter and lemon zest in a food processor until the mixture is creamy. Put into a large bowl and beat in the flour to form a stiff dough.

Roll out thinly on a lightly floured surface and stamp out biscuits using an attractive cutter (I like heart shapes). Transfer to the prepared baking sheet and bake in the middle of the oven for 8–12 minutes until golden around the edges. Transfer to a wire cooling rack. Mix together the sugar and thyme and sprinkle over the shortbread. Serve when they are cool and crisp.

Makes 30–40 biscuits, depending on the size of the cutter

Preparation: 25 mins
Cooking: 12 mins

FRUIT TARTS WITH HERBS

Apple, pear or other fruit tarts can be made simply by arranging sliced fruit on a pastry base, adding a few finely chopped herbs and spooning apple jelly flavoured with the same herb on top. No sugar is needed because the jelly is quite sweet enough and acts as a perfect glaze. For this recipe I have used a jelly flavoured with lemon thyme and sprinkled more thyme leaves over the top, but this works equally well with an apple and rosemary jelly, sprinkled with fresh rosemary. Another favourite is to make the tart with redcurrants and add finely chopped fresh hyssop, which makes such a lovely combination. Cover the fruit and herb with redcurrant jelly and bake as below.

1 sheet of ready-rolled puff pastry
3 pears, peeled, cored and sliced
2 tsp chopped lemon thyme leaves
½ recipe quantity Apple and Herb Jelly (see page
  166), made with lemon thyme

Preheat the oven to 180°C/350°F/Gas 4 and grease a baking sheet.

Put the pastry on the prepared baking sheet and cover with the pears, sprinkle with the thyme, then spoon the jelly on top. Bake for 20 minutes, then serve hot or cold.

Serves 4

Preparation: 10 mins
Cooking: 20 mins

HERB SUGARS AND SYRUPS

Herb sugars and syrups are the unsung heroes of ice creams, sorbets, cocktails, cakes, fruit dishes and many other desserts. They were popular in Britain with Victorian cooks, but sank into oblivion until recently. Now with more people buying and growing herbs, syrups and sugars are being made again to add sweetness and personality to food and drinks.

HERB SYRUPS

Bay syrup enriches the flavour of poached pears, hyssop complements peaches and strawberries, and lemon verbena or sweet cicely syrups are perfect with melon. Pannacotta becomes memorable when it is made with lavender or thyme syrups. You'll see how my cake recipes – Rose Cake (see page 109) and Apple and Rosemary Cake (see page 213) – are improved by soaking in herb syrups. I once had some early English strawberries which were not ripe enough to have a full flavour. So I served them in individual bowls with a pannacotta and a French madeleine soaked in rosemary syrup. The experiment was a great success. If you are making herb syrups it can save time to start with some stock syrup.

STOCK SYRUP FOR HERBS
225g/8oz/heaped 1 cup sugar
300ml/10½fl oz/1¼ cups water

Dissolve the sugar in the water over a low heat and then bring to the boil for 2 minutes. Allow to cool. This will keep in the refrigerator for at least one week.

Makes about 400ml/14fl oz/1¾ cups

MINT SYRUP
Boil 4 sprigs of fresh mint with 400ml/14fl oz/1¾ cups of syrup for 5 minutes, then strain. I use apple, pineapple, spearmint or Bowles's mint for the best flavours.

LAVENDER SYRUP
Make this syrup when the lavender flowers are in bud and use 1 tablespoon of lavender buds to 400ml/14fl oz/ 1¾ cups of syrup. Boil up and strain, as above.

SCENTED GERANIUM SYRUP
Use four leaves to 400ml/14fl oz/1¾ cups of syrup and prepare as above. Attar of Roses is my most useful culinary geranium with its rose-scented leaves. It won the RHS Award of Merit, which will not surprise you when you rub the leaves and enjoy the wonderful aroma. There are other geraniums which have leaves with pineapple, lemon, cedar, nutmeg or floral scents.

LOVAGE SYRUP
Use a small handful of lovage leaves to 400ml/ 14fl oz/1¾ cups of syrup and prepare as above. This can be used as the basis of a gin cocktail (see page 132).

HERB SUGARS

Sugars are easy to make when herbs are at their freshest. And they are a simple method of adding subtle herb flavours to many recipes, including sorbets, biscuits and cream-based puddings. Fill an attractive jar with 450g/1lb/2¼ cups of sugar with 115g/4oz herb tucked in. In about 2 weeks, the flavour will be sucked up into the sugar. But I leave the herbs in the sugars for up to a year, when they are usually used up, and my herbs are again at their freshest for making more.

I have found that lavender buds and small herb leaves mix up too much with the sugar, and need sieving out before using the scented sugar. So I now wrap them in muslin/cheesecloth before adding to the jar. Try scented geranium leaves, rose petals, rosemary, thyme, bay, lavender, pineapple sage, lemon verbena or calamint.

Use 3 bay leaves or 115g/4oz of lavender buds, chopped rosemary or scented geranium in 450g/1lb/2¼ cups of sugar. Leave for at least 2 weeks.

You can get an instant result by pounding herbs with sugar in a pestle and mortar until the herb leaves disintegrate to colour and flavour the sugar (see page 152 for pineapple sage sugar). To make lemon verbena sugar, pound 3 tablespoons of finely chopped young leaves with the same amount of sugar until you have a fine, pale green mixture. Use herb sugars made in this way quickly as the flavour soon fades. You can use caster/superfine or granulated sugar, white or golden. Sugar cubes/lumps are particularly effective in making herb sugars this way.

[WHY NOT TRY...]

+ Using herb syrups as a cordial with ice cubes and soda
+ Making sponge cakes with scented geranium sugar
+ Adding rosemary syrup to crème brûlée or ice cream recipes

GRIDDLED PINEAPPLE WITH CHILLI AND ROSEMARY SYRUP

This looks inviting on the plate and tastes exotic with its three powerful flavours of pineapple, chilli and rosemary.

280g/10oz/scant 1½ cups caster/superfine sugar
1 lime, thinly sliced
1 red chilli, deseeded and chopped
4 tbsp chopped rosemary leaves
1 large pineapple

Make the syrup first by dissolving the sugar in 500ml/17fl oz/generous 2 cups water, then turn up the heat and boil the sugar syrup for 2 minutes. Add the lime, chilli and rosemary, bring back to the boil and cook for another 5 minutes. Peel and slice the pineapple and cook in a hot griddle pan, hot enough to create a criss-cross pattern on both sides of the pineapple slices. Put in a large, shallow dish and pour over the syrup. Leave overnight to allow the flavours to infuse. Serve chilled.

Serves 4   Preparation: 10 mins   Cook: 15 mins, plus chilling

LOVAGE AND GIN FIZZ

I like to sip this exciting combination in the garden on a perfect summer evening. If you plan ahead you can make ice cubes with a small lovage leaf frozen inside each one. You can also make a lovage gin and tonic by macerating gin with bruised lovage leaves for 2 days.

FOR EACH COCKTAIL
2 tbsp Lovage Syrup (see page 130)
3 tbsp gin
1 tbsp lemon or lime juice
125ml/4fl oz/½ cup soda water, to serve
ice cubes and a lovage leaf, to serve

Shake the syrup, gin and juice together in a cocktail shaker. Sieve into a glass over ice and top up with soda water.

Preparation: 5 mins

AUTUMN

AUTUMN HERBS

In early autumn, my herb garden is still full of flowers and the insects that love them. I have marjoram, oregano, calamint, anise, hyssop and the vibrant nasturtiums and pot marigolds in bloom. Herbs should play a part in herbaceous borders too, because so many other garden plants have finished flowering.

When the herbs eventually have to be harvested, I dry the flowers for pot pourri and dry leaves of mint, lemon balm, thyme and oregano to be stored in airtight jars for cooking and for making herb teas. The seeds of chervil, sorrel, lovage, sweet cicely, fennel, dill and hyssop are saved and dried. Some are used in cooking and all are sown in autumn or spring to produce more herbs. I also save the seeds of salad herbs to sow in the spring.

By early autumn I have clipped the lavender and dried its flower stems. I also cut back the long hedges of winter savory and wall germander, keeping some of the clippings to take hardwood cuttings. I also take cuttings from rosemary, thyme, tarragon and lavender.

To take successful cuttings, fill a pot with well-draining cutting compost, made by mixing sand with potting compost. Firm the compost just below the rim and water well. Do not overcrowd the pot with cuttings and keep to one type of herb, as they vary in how long they take to form roots.

Choose sturdy non-flowering shoots with plenty of leaves. Use a very sharp knife and cut the base of the stem just below a node, leaving a shoot of 10–13cm/ 4–5in. Remove the leaves at the bottom of the stem, leaving at least two leaves at the top which are needed to feed the plant as it produces roots.

Make a hole in the compost with a pencil or dibber and dip the stem in hormone rooting powder before putting it in the hole. I put the cuttings around the edge of the pot, making sure the leaves do not touch the compost as this can cause fungal infections; the rooting powder helps prevent this because it contains plant hormones and fungicide. Terracotta pots are more successful than plastic pots in my experience.

Label and date and put the pot in a propagator, or cover with a plastic bag which is kept from touching the leaves by using a simple hoop or frame. Keep out of the hot sun. Only water from below and do it in the mornings, not at night. Check for roots after three or four weeks by giving the stem a gentle tug. If it resists, you can celebrate the creation of a new herb plant.

Before the first frosts, I take the half-hardy herbs – like the scented geraniums, pineapple, tangerine and blackcurrant sages, lemon verbena and tricolour sage – into the greenhouse in their pots. I also put tarragon, mint and chives in pots to overwinter in the greenhouse, so they are ready for the kitchen before the same herbs growing in the garden.

I harvest basil and other herbs that will disappear underground in the winter. These are used to make pesto, tapenades, herb butters, sauces and soups. Others go in chutneys and spiced fruits, herb oils, vinegars and herb and apple jellies. This is the season when I harvest orchard fruits and autumn vegetables, like courgettes/zucchini and pumpkins, to cook with a variety of herbs.

The salad herbs I planted for winter use and the clumps of herbs, like garlic chives, marjoram and lovage, will need thinning. Then after a final weed I use my own compost on the beds, except in the areas where Mediterranean herbs like thyme and hyssop thrive in poor, free-draining soil. In early autumn, I sow more chervil and coriander/cilantro seeds. The chervil likes shady areas, so I plant it along the north wall where my mints thrive.

Collect seeds on a dry day and store in paper bags or large old envelopes in a dry place. With seed heads like lovage and fennel, hang them upside down in a paper bag tied lightly around the seed heads, so that the seeds dry and fall into the bag. Seeds will normally be ready within three weeks. When you harvest your herbs like oregano to dry for winter use, do not forget to harvest soft herbs too. But delicate herbs like dill, chives and tarragon will have to be frozen in water or oil in ice cube trays.

In late autumn, tidy up the herb area, removing dried up annuals like borage, coriander/cilantro or dill, saving seeds to dry and re-use. Autumn is the time to sow lovage, angelica, chamomile and fennel seeds outside. I leave seed heads on herbs like garlic chives and agastache. They look attractive and finches love the seeds for lunch.

In the meantime, we lunch on autumn herbs like parsley, sage, sorrel, chervil, fennel, hyssop and marjoram. All the hard herbs like bay, rosemary, savory and thyme are also being used constantly in the kitchen. With a large, mixed orchard it is a very busy time, making several different herb jellies, spiced pears, plums and damsons and many different conserves (see pages 166–7).

It is time to deal with the unruly mint, which inevitably has invaded herb beds and threatened less thuggish species. The real rogues are Bowles's mint, spearmint and Moroccan mint. They have to be dug up, root cuttings taken and many new mint plants produced. After problems with them in the herb garden, I put these three thugs in a large metal farm drinking trough and divided it into three with metal sheets. They each had their own area, which they kept to for a couple of years. Then one of them took over the whole trough, proving which mint is the biggest bully of all. It was Bowles's mint, which ironically has a very subtle taste in mint tea and mint sauce.

[AUTUMN ACTION LIST]

+ Cut back on watering herbs grown in containers.
+ Protect plants like bay and myrtles in outside containers with fleece or hessian and, if possible, move them to a south-facing wall for the winter.
+ Sow parsley seed inside with heat.
+ Take root cuttings of tarragon.
+ Divide herbs like marjoram, oregano, lovage, sorrel, chives, lemon balm and bergamot.

PARSLEY

Parsley is definitely the most widely used herb around the world. But too many cooks use it automatically day after day, finding it useful but not always inspiring. It is often used as a finishing touch to food, as the worst kind of decoration, with no link to the dish lying beneath its chopped leaves. This is an unkind fate for a herb with an interesting, aromatic flavour, which is an integral ingredient in many delicious international dishes.

HISTORY

Parsley is native to the Mediterranean, but soon spread to the rest of Europe and gradually to most parts of the world. Parsley is a merger of the Old English *petersilie* and the Old French *peresil*, both derived from medieval Latin. This herb was once associated with death and in Ancient Greece it was used to decorate tombs. The Ancient Romans had a different idea. They not only ate parsley in vast quantities but they made it into garlands for their guests, to discourage drunkenness and also to deter unpleasantly strong smells.

COOKING

Every year I grow flatleaf, curly and par-cel parsley, but occasionally I also try Hamburg parsley, which is grown for its root and, unlike other parsley, is not a leaf crop at all. The best parsley for taste is flatleaf parsley, which is used in vast quantities in Middle Eastern and Asian recipes. That is why huge bunches of flatleaf parsley are on sale at Indian shops and in areas of most cities where there are a lot of Turkish, Lebanese, Algerian, Moroccan or Tunisian restaurants. Italian and Greek recipes include a lot of flatleaf parsley, too.

I use it in sauces like Sauce Verte, Salsa Verdi, Chimichurri Sauce and my favourite for serving with Osso Buco – Gremolata. They are all described on pages 142–3. Parsley is excellent in sauces served with fish and seafood. Many Middle Eastern recipes demand flatleaf parsley chopped finely with mint, like the Tabbouleh recipe on page 60. It is a relief to me that I have it growing in the herb garden throughout the year.

Curly parsley is often served chopped finely on potatoes and other vegetables, but when I have a lot, I make Classic Pesto (see page 35) and onion and parsley soup. Another herb I grow is called par-cel or leaf celery. It looks like large, tough parsley and can grow to 30cm/12in tall. The taste is a mix of celery and parsley and I always use it in cooked dishes because of its slight toughness.

GROWING

Growing parsley is said to be difficult and there are lots of myths, including the belief that you would get the best crops if you planted on Good Friday and that if you had success with parsley in your garden you were probably a witch, or at least a bossy wife.

I ignore all of this and make three sowings a year. I plant seeds inside in late winter to give me a head start on plants grown in the garden. When they germinate, which takes some time, I pot them on and soon plant them outside in the herb garden about 13cm/5in apart. It is possible to put three seedlings into one pot and then grow them together as one bushy plant. I also sow seeds directly into the ground in spring and then later in early summer, for plants that will grow through the winter.

Parsley likes to be planted deep into moist, fertile soil. It is happy in pots and window boxes if you keep it well watered. You can also use it, as I do, as an edging to beds of herbs or flowers. It is a hardy biennial, which survives bad frosts. In late spring parsley can bolt if it gets too dry. It will help to remove flowering stems and water the plants well. This will extend the period when you will have harvestable leaves.

Once parsley flowers become seed heads, the plants are coming to the end of their useful life and there will be few leaves available. But you will have new plants growing inside if you follow my plan of sowing three times a year; parsley that should be ready to put out in the garden. Parsley thrives in a sunny, moist position, although it does tolerate light summer shade.

OSSO BUCO WITH GREMOLATA

75g/2½oz/scant ½ cup plain/all-purpose flour

4 pieces of veal shin (or pork or beef), ideally 5cm/2in thick

55g/2oz/¼ cup butter

1 onion, finely chopped

2 celery stalks, finely chopped

1 large garlic clove, finely chopped

3 salted anchovies

180ml/6fl oz/¾ cup dry white wine

180ml/6fl oz/¾ cup vegetable stock

600g/1lb 5oz tomatoes, skinned, deseeded and chopped (see page 24), about 250g/9oz prepared weight

sea salt and freshly ground black pepper

1 recipe quantity Gremolata (see page 142), to serve

grated Parmesan cheese, to serve

Risotto alla Milanese

1 recipe quantity Basic Risotto (see page 184)

½ tsp saffron strands

Osso buco is Italian for "bone with a hole", because the slices of veal shin used have a hole in the bone filled with delicious bone marrow. We celebrated our younger son's engagement by having dinner at St John in London, which specializes in using every part of the animal and serves bone marrow with parsley salad as a first course. But I was shocked when our son announced he was trying bone marrow for the first time ever "because the doctors harvested so much of my own bone marrow when I was being treated for leukaemia". A reaction typical of his excellent, though unusual, sense of humour.

Preheat the oven to 180°C/350°F/Gas 4. Season the flour with salt and pepper, then coat the meat in the flour. Heat the butter in a heavy-based, flameproof casserole dish large enough for the pieces of meat to fit in one layer. Brown and seal the meat on both sides. Remove and, using the same pan, gently fry the onion and celery for about 10 minutes until they soften, then add the garlic and anchovies. Stir until the anchovies have melted. Add the wine, stock and tomatoes. Bring to the boil and simmer until the sauce has reduced to leave enough to cover the meat when the pieces are put back into the pan. They should be carefully placed so that the marrow cannot fall out during cooking.

Cover with baking parchment and then the lid. Cook in the oven for at least 2 hours, until the meat is tender and the sauce has thickened, checking on it occasionally. It can be left in a very low oven when it has finished cooking.

When the meat is almost ready, make the risotto following the instructions on page 184, adding the saffron with the stock and continuing until the risotto is creamy. Spread each piece of osso buco with the gremolata before serving with the risotto alla Milanese and extra Parmesan cheese.

Serves 4

Preparation: 45 mins
Cooking: 2–3 hrs

PARSLEY SAUCES

GREMOLATA

This is the Italian garnish of finely chopped parsley and garlic mixed with lemon zest. It adds a fresh, citrus note, a final flourish, to lift rich, meaty dishes like Osso Buco. If you do not like raw garlic, shallots can be used instead. With gremolata, the whole is definitely greater than the sum of its parts. Garlic, parsley and lemon are common ingredients around the kitchen, but when they are finely chopped together they become something very special, adding vitality to this dish and to many others. The parsley gives a fresh, clean taste; the garlic, which must be very fresh, brings oomph; and the lemon zest adds acid and zip. Gremolata is part condiment, part garnish, and it adds a bright freshness to other meat dishes, like lamb and chicken. I also use it with fish, creamy bean dishes, pasta and cooked vegetables, especially asparagus. Adding lemon juice to cooked vegetables can dull the normal green colour, but the lemon zest does not react in the same way, leaving you with a bright lemon taste on bright green vegetables.

1 small handful of flatleaf parsley, leaves picked
   and finely chopped
2 garlic cloves, finely chopped
grated zest of 2 lemons

Mix together the parsley leaves, garlic and lemon zest.

Serves 4

SALSA VERDE

This parsley sauce is so versatile, it can be served with meat, fish, poultry, pasta, goats' cheese and cooked vegetables. It is good to have around to lift recipes and will keep in a jar in the refrigerator for several days. This is the basic recipe but you can add a chopped chilli if you want a spicy salsa. And there are dozens of different salsas that work well. Try mango, chilli and coriander/cilantro, or red onion, tomato and chives. Make this recipe first and then experiment.

1 large handful of flatleaf parsley, leaves picked
   and chopped
2 garlic cloves, crushed
1 tbsp Dijon mustard
6 anchovies, rinsed (optional)
2 tbsp capers, drained and rinsed
grated zest and juice of 1 lemon
150ml/5fl oz/scant ⅔ cup olive oil
sea salt and freshly ground black pepper

This salsa is traditionally made in a pestle and mortar but I normally put all the ingredients apart from the lemon juice and oil into a food processor for about 5 minutes until they are well blended. Then, with the motor running, pour in the oil slowly until the mixture thickens to become an attractive green purée. I pep it up with the lemon juice and finally season with salt and pepper to taste.

Serves 4

Preparation: 15 mins

Preparation: 15 mins

SAUCE VERTE

This parsley-based sauce is traditionally served with cold salmon but it is also good with other fish and vegetables. It is basically a green herb mayonnaise. Make your own mayonnaise using the recipe for Chive Mayonnaise (see page 32) or use a good quality shop-bought one.

100g/3½oz fresh, young spinach leaves
40g/1½oz flatleaf parsley, leaves picked
4 tbsp chopped tarragon leaves (optional)
150ml/5fl oz/scant ⅔ cup mayonnaise
juice of about ½ lemon
sea salt and freshly ground black pepper

Rinse the spinach and parsley leaves, and the tarragon leaves, if using, then put them in a large saucepan with just the water clinging to the leaves. Place over a medium heat and leave to wilt for 2–3 minutes. Rinse in cold water again to keep the fresh, green colour and then squeeze out any moisture using a wooden spoon and a sieve. This is very important.

Put the leaves into a food processor with the mayonnaise. Season with salt and pepper and blend until you have a smooth, green sauce. Add lemon juice to taste.

Serves 4

Preparation: 25 mins
Cooking: 3 mins

CHIMICHURRI SAUCE

Chimichurri is a green sauce that originated in Argentina, where people love to get together to eat and chat. And grilled/broiled or fried beef served with this spicy sauce is one of their favourite recipes for a social occasion. The name of the sauce is thought to be a Basque word, which means a "mixture of several things". Spaniards from the Basque region settled in Argentina in the late 19th century. A red version of this sauce can be made by adding tomato and red pepper to the mix for blending. I like to serve it with sirloin, the tastiest of steaks – brushed with oil and cooked in a seriously hot pan for a couple of minutes on each side.

1 large handful of flatleaf parsley, leaves picked
  and chopped
1 tbsp chopped oregano or ½ tbsp dried
2 shallots
1 small green chilli, deseeded and chopped
4 garlic cloves
4 tbsp olive oil
juice of 1 lime
4 tbsp sherry vinegar
sea salt and freshly ground black pepper

Blend the herbs, shallots, chilli and garlic in a food processor. Add the oil, lime juice and vinegar, season with salt and pepper and blend again.

Serves 4

Preparation: 15 mins

MUSSELS, PARSLEY, CHILLI AND SQUID INK PASTA

This dish looks stunning and sophisticated on white plates with the black of the pasta mixed with the green parsley, the pale orange mussels and red spots of chopped chilli. It can, of course, be made without the heat of the chilli for a more gentle recipe. If you are a real enthusiast, you can make your own squid ink pasta for this dish. I only tried it once in my pasta maker. I ordered the right amount of deep black cuttlefish ink from our local fishmonger and followed the pasta recipe closely. I hung up the fettuccine to dry on the back of a chair only to be told by my husband that it looked like a very dirty, grey string vest. It did, however, taste deliciously fishy. I now prefer to buy blacker-than-black squid ink pasta, which makes this dish look beautiful every time I serve it.

1.5 kg/3lb 5oz mussels in their shells, scrubbed and bearded
2 tbsp olive oil
1 shallot, finely chopped
2 garlic cloves, finely chopped
1 red chilli, deseeded and chopped
120ml/4fl oz/½ cup dry white wine
400g/14oz black spaghetti, fettuccine or similar pasta
4 tbsp chopped flatleaf parsley leaves
sea salt and freshly ground black pepper

Preparation: 45 mins
Cooking: 22 mins

Rinse the cleaned mussels well and discard any that remain open when given a sharp tap. Put them in a large, heavy-based pan with just enough water to cover the base of the pan, cover and bring to the boil over a high heat. Cook for a few minutes until the mussels open, shaking the pan occasionally and discarding any mussels that remain closed. Leave until they are cool enough to take out of their shells if you are planning to serve them this way. Strain the small amount of liquid and keep to one side.

Heat the oil in a frying pan over a medium heat and fry the shallot for about 8 minutes until it softens, then add the garlic and chilli and stir. Add the wine and the liquid from the mussels. Boil until the sauce has reduced to 3–4 tablespoons, then add the mussels, either removed from their shells or left in for serving.

Meanwhile, cook the pasta in boiling water until al dente, then drain and add it to the mussel mixture in the pan. Stir well. Season with salt and pepper and serve scattered with the chopped parsley.

Serves 4

HERB OILS AND VINEGARS

Herb oils and vinegars are an attractive way of preserving the flavour of herbs and then using them in salad dressings, marinades, for drizzling over food and for stir-fry dishes. I store bottles in my larder for my own use and they also make popular presents. I collect beautiful bottles to make oils and vinegars in, then label and decorate with a ribbon tied around a bunch of the fresh herb.

HERB OILS

I like using the hard herbs – bay, thyme, rosemary and savory – with a few dried chillies, the number depending on the size of the bottle of oil. This oil is known as my Hot Herb Oil and it is very popular with friends. They tend to say: "Please come to dinner – and would you mind bringing some more of your wonderful herb and chilli oil? Oh and bring your husband, too."

Fill a jar with extra virgin olive oil and then put in four sprigs of washed and dried herb. You can make it with a mixture of herbs, but making an oil with only one type really captures its taste. Hard herbs are easy to use and for bay use 8–10 leaves. But you can also make herb oils with the softer herbs like basil, dill, fennel and mint. And you can use dried peppercorns in a spicy oil or make flavoured oils using coriander, fennel or dill seeds.

Herb oils will keep for up to year if stored in a cool, dark place. There is said to be a very slight risk of botulism from storing herb oils for a long time, because the spores of the bacterium which causes botulism can be present on anything that grows in soil, including herbs. One way to reduce any risk is to avoid using garlic, and to strain the oil to remove the herbs after two weeks. Then store the bottle of oil in a cool, dark place. Some

people even keep their herb oils in the refrigerator to reduce the risk, while others believe that adding a little lemon juice helps. But I have to say that I have been making herb oils for decades, leaving in the herbs and keeping them dark but not refrigerator-cool. There has never been a problem.

BASIL OIL

This is an excellent way of capturing the unique and useful flavour of basil. You will need 5 tablespoons of basil leaves for 500ml/17fl oz/generous 2 cups of olive oil. Remove the leaves of the basil and pound them in a mortar. Add some oil and pound again to bruise the leaves so they release their own oil. Mix with the rest of the oil, pour into a jar and put it in a sunny spot, shaking regularly for two weeks. Then strain the oil into an attractive bottle, add a few fresh leaves to help identify the oil and store in a dark, cool place.

CHIVE OIL

Chive oil can be made in the same way as basil oil, using 7 tablespoons of snipped chives in place of the basil. I have just used some drops of chive oil, given to me by the food expert Lyn Hall, on a clear tomato soup, which I then served sprinkled with chopped young chives.

HERB VINEGARS

Herb vinegars look so beautiful and are simple to make. Put your chosen herb into an attractive bottle, fill with good-quality white wine vinegar or cider vinegar and leave in a sunny place for two weeks. Then strain and put the vinegar back into the bottle with a fresh sprig of the herb. Store for your own use or give to a lucky friend.

Most herb experts make vinegars as I do, but a few believe in crushing the herbs in a pestle and mortar, boiling a little of the vinegar and pounding the herbs again in this hot vinegar. It is then cooled and mixed with the rest of the vinegar and stored for two weeks. After straining the herb vinegar, the clear liquid can be stored in a clean jar for at least two years.

Tarragon vinegar is the classic choice, but in the winter when my tarragon is still underground I make a chervil vinegar which provides the same aniseed flavour and has subtle, feathery leaves which look good in the bottle. Another good-looker is chive vinegar made when the herb is coming into flower. A few stalks with flower buds can be tied together in the wine vinegar. Also try rose petal, dill, fennel, lovage, mint, oregano, sage, savory, rosemary, thyme or nasturtium vinegars.

SALAD BURNET VINEGAR

I make salad burnet vinegar in the winter, when this attractive, cucumber-tasting herb is thriving in the herb garden. This has been popular since Victorian days and I often make it for my herb cookery school because its leaves are exceptionally pretty and it has a mild cucumber taste that is perfect for making a dressing for cucumber salad. Pack the leaves into a litre bottle of good-quality white wine vinegar. Leave for 2 weeks, strain and put into a fresh jar with two sprigs of burnet.

ROSE PETAL VINEGAR

Make a special vinegar by adding the petals of 6 roses, 1 dried chilli and the zest of 1 lemon to 500ml/17fl oz/ generous 2 cups of white wine vinegar. It is ready to use after leaving by a window for 5 days.

ROSE GERANIUM VINEGAR

I make a delightful vinegar with rose-scented geranium leaves mixed with raspberries and wine vinegar. Roughly crush 6 rose-scented geranium leaves and 400g/14oz/3 cups raspberries in a food processor. Pour over 250ml/9fl oz/generous 1 cup white wine vinegar and leave in the refrigerator, stirring occasionally, for 5 days. Then put the mixture in a jelly bag and drip into a bowl overnight. Put the strained liquid in a saucepan, add 175g/6oz/heaped ¾ cup sugar and heat slowly until it has dissolved. Bring to the boil for 10 minutes. Cool, removing all the scum. Put the cold vinegar into bottles and use within a year.

[WHY NOT TRY...]

+ Making marinades for fish and meat using herb oils and vinegars when the herb is out of season – dill and fennel for fish or chicken; oregano with lamb; thyme for beef and added to orange juice with duck; rosemary with beef or lamb; coriander/cilantro with grated ginger; garlic and chilli with fish and seafood
+ Drizzling herb oil onto freshly cooked pasta and finishing with a little Parmesan and plenty of black pepper
+ Serving small bowls of herb oils and vinegars with chunks of good sourdough bread for dipping
+ Experimenting with your own flavour combinations; add spice seeds, pared and dried citrus zest, or chillies – from hot cayenne to smoky chipotle – to the bottle

SAGE

Hard herbs, like sage, bay, savory and rosemary, add shape and interest to the garden and are invaluable in the kitchen, too. I am so fond of sage that I grow nine different *Salvia* species – common sage, broad-leaf, gold, purple, Tricolor, white, pineapple, tangerine and blackcurrant. But in this large Labiatae family there are in fact over 750 species around the world, made up of annuals, biennials and perennials.

HISTORY

Sage is native to the Mediterranean and its name is derived from the Latin word *salveo*, which means to save, cure or heal. It was used by the Ancient Greeks, Romans and Chinese for almost all medical conditions, but before the days of refrigeration it was also used to preserve or cure meat. It helps us to digest fatty meats like pork and liver, balancing the richness of many dishes. It is also good in cooked cheese recipes and is famously used to flavour Sage Derby cheese.

COOKING

Although sage can be dried, it always tastes much better fresh, with its spicy, slightly bitter flavour. My favourite sage leaves for taste are from common sage, but all of my nine different sages are worth eating.

I have recently started to use sage to make Strong Herb Pesto (see page 35) and sage tea, and I make pickled apple in the autumn by using sage in the Spiced Fruit on page 167. Sage is essential to many stuffing recipes, including one with apple and pickled walnuts to serve with the Christmas goose and another with apricot and celery stuffing for turkey. Sage is also good deep-fried with calves' liver or cooked with pork on a bed of apple, garlic and onion. But perhaps my favourite is Veal Saltimbocca (see page 156).

GROWING

As it is easy to train common sage and purple sage into attractive circular bushes, I use them to highlight the corners of my herb beds. The vibrant blue flowers are an important part of the garden during the summer, when they are a magnet for bees and butterflies. It is very important to cut them back hard after flowering to encourage new, fresh leaves to form well before winter.

I first grew white sage from seed and now have several plants in the herb garden, which earn their keep because the white flowers are beautiful and the narrow, grey leaves can be used in cooking. Broad-leaf sage makes a bold statement in the garden, growing around a huge pot of lemon verbena. I was given my first plant as a cutting from the head gardener at Barnsley House, the famous Cotswold garden created by Rosemary Verey, the English garden designer. The pale blue flowers are pretty amongst the large grey-green leaves.

Tricolor sage is an attractive sage with its leaves showing pink, white, purple and green colouring. As it is half-hardy, I bring it into the greenhouse for the winter. It has a mild flavour for cooking, looks great on the plate, but can only be grown from cuttings.

The scented sage plants – pineapple, tangerine and blackcurrant – are also half-hardy. If you have space for them on a windowsill, they repay you by giving off a glorious scent of the fruit and producing useful leaves through the year. When you crush the leaves in your fingers you will be rewarded by an astonishingly strong aroma. All three sages can only be grown from cuttings and produce attractive flowers for many months. I use them to make herb teas (see page 46) and syrups.

Take sage softwood cuttings in late spring and early summer, choosing healthy new growth. Larger plants will often root naturally, making it easy to establish new plants. White and common sage, which can be grown from seed, should be sown in trays with vermiculite in spring. They usually germinate within a month.

Sage plants enjoy warm, dry soil. They do not like to be cut back later than mid-summer; autumn pruning can kill a plant. Sages can become woody after several years, so grow new plants to replace them when necessary.

PINEAPPLE SAGE WITH AUTUMN RASPBERRIES AND MASCARPONE

This is a marvellous combination of the intense pineapple taste of the sage, the deep flavour of autumn raspberries and the creamy mascarpone. You can use granulated sugar as I do, but if you have sugar cubes/lumps in the house do use them because crushing the cubes/lumps helps the pineapple sage leaves to disintegrate. When you decorate the pudding with a sprig of fresh pineapple sage, it is a bonus if the sage is in flower. Then you can add a few whole raspberries to the top to match the red petals of the herb flowers.

1 handful of pineapple sage leaves, plus 4 sprigs to decorate
85g/3oz/scant ½ cup granulated sugar
250g/9oz/heaped 1 cup mascarpone cheese
400g/14oz/3 cups autumn raspberries

Choose young, bright green leaves from the pineapple sage and put them into a mortar or bowl with the sugar. Pound the sugar and herb together with a pestle or the end of a rolling pin. The sage will soon disintegrate, turning the sugar green.

Mix the sage sugar with the mascarpone, then gently fold in the raspberries. Divide into four attractive glass dishes and serve with a sprig of pineapple sage on top.

Serves 4

Preparation: 15 mins

BAKED AUBERGINE WITH SAGE PESTO AND FRIED SAGE LEAVES

This is one of the easiest ways of cooking aubergine/eggplant. Its flavour is lifted by the sage and the fresh tomato sauce. These vegetables used to be so bitter that it was wise to salt them to remove the strong juices. But today the bitterness has been bred out of them, so there is no need to salt aubergines being roasted or grilled/broiled, only if they are being fried. Then sprinkle on salt, leave them to disgorge their juices, rinse and pat dry.

2 large aubergines/eggplants
4 tbsp olive oil
1 recipe quantity Strong Herb
   Pesto made with sage
   (see page 35)
1 recipe quantity Tomato Sauce
   (see page 68), omitting the
   oregano
120ml/4fl oz/½ cup olive oil,
   for frying
16 sage leaves
2 lemons, cut into wedges
sea salt and freshly ground
   black pepper

Preheat the oven to 220°C/425°F/Gas 7. Cut the aubergine/eggplant in half lengthways, through the stalk. Make a deep, crisscross pattern across the cut surface with a small, sharp knife. Pour 1 tablespoon of oil onto each aubergine/eggplant half, season with salt and pepper and bake in the oven for about 25 minutes. The flesh should then be soft.

Preheat the grill/broiler. Spread the pesto over the scored surfaces of the cooked aubergines/eggplants. Grill/broil until it is bubbling. Meanwhile, gently heat up the tomato sauce.

Heat the frying oil to 180°C/350°F in a heavy-based saucepan. (If you don't have a thermometer, carefully lower in a wooden spoon handle and the oil should bubble around it.) The oil should start to swirl on top. This is the time to drop in the sage leaves and fry for about 30 seconds until they are crisp. Remove with a slotted spoon and drain on paper towels. Serve the aubergines/eggplants with the tomato sauce, lemon wedges for squeezing and the fried sage leaves.

Serves 4

Preparation: 30 mins
Cooking: 45 mins

SAGE AND GARLIC ROAST PORK BELLY WITH POWER PLUM SAUCE

2kg/4lb 8oz pork belly on the bone
1 tbsp very finely chopped sage leaves
4 garlic cloves, crushed
sea salt and freshly ground black pepper
potatoes and a green vegetable, to serve

POWER PLUM SAUCE
1 large sharp eating/dessert apple or cooking apple, peeled, cored and chopped
350g/12oz plums, pitted
10 sage leaves, finely chopped
225g/8oz/1½ cups dried apricots
185g/6½oz/scant 1 cup caster/ superfine sugar, plus extra if needed
150ml/5fl oz/scant ⅔ cup white wine vinegar
1 red chilli, deseeded and chopped

This is a spicy, thick sauce that enlivens roast pork or duck and spare ribs. It is also good with terrines, cold meats and cheese. You can make it in advance whenever you have plenty of plums and store it in sterilized jars (see page 166) so it's ready for this recipe, or simply prepare it while you wait for the pork to slow cook.

Preheat the oven to 220°C/425°F/Gas 7. Pat the pork belly dry with paper towels and score the skin. Season the pork, rubbing the salt into the skin. Make a paste of the sage and garlic in a pestle and mortar, then rub it over the pork. Roast the pork for 30 minutes, then lower the heat to 180°C/350°F/Gas 4 and continue to cook for a further 1½ hours.

Meanwhile, make the sauce. Cook the apple with 6 tablespoons of water for about 10 minutes until soft, then add all the other ingredients. Simmer until thick. This normally takes at least 45 minutes. Taste and add more sugar, if necessary.

Smear about 2 tablespoons of the sauce over the surface of the pork and continue roasting for a further 30 minutes until the skin is crisp and the meat very tender.

Serve the pork belly with the remaining sauce (cold or reheated, if you like), potatoes and a green vegetable.

Serves 4

Preparation: 25 mins
Cooking: 2½ hrs

VEAL SALTIMBOCCA

This authentic Italian recipe uses veal, but it can also be made with pork tenderloin medallions for anyone who does not eat veal. However, chefs in Rome, where it originated, would not approve.

4 slices of veal escalope, about
   115g/4oz each
4 slices of Parma ham/
   prosciutto
8 sage leaves
2 tbsp olive oil
240ml/8fl oz/1 cup Marsala
freshly ground black pepper
spinach and new potatoes,
   to serve

Grind black pepper onto the veal and wrap a slice of ham around each escalope. Place 2 sage leaves on the top of each piece, fastening the leaves and ham in place with cocktail sticks/toothpicks.

Heat the oil in a large frying pan and fry the veal over a high heat for 2 minutes on each side, starting with the sage-leaf side. Transfer the veal to warm serving plates.

Pour the Marsala into the hot pan and allow it to reduce until it becomes syrupy, then pour it over the veal and serve with spinach and new potatoes.

Serves 4

Preparation: 20 mins
Cooking: 10 mins

SORREL

Of all the 150 different culinary herbs I grow, sorrel is the one used most often in my cooking. I grow three types of sorrel and also occasionally pick wild sorrel, known as Sour Sally, with its sharp-tasting, narrow, spear-like leaves. Common or broad-leaf sorrel, *Rumex acetosa*, edges a large bed in the herb garden, growing to about 30cm/12in tall. I pick it most days for soups, sauces, salads, tarts and terrines.

Buckler-leaf sorrel, *Rumex scutatus*, is also used regularly in salads. It has attractive small leaves, shaped like shields, which have a mild, lemony taste. A favourite salad is made up of these leaves mixed with small new potatoes, capers, lemon zest and a mustardy salad dressing, which I serve with fish or chicken (see page 162). I also grow red-veined sorrel, which earns a place on the plate because of its glamorous looks. But in the taste stakes it does not compare to broad-leaf and buckler-leaf sorrels.

HISTORY

Sorrel is native to Asia, North America and Europe. It was first enjoyed as far back as 3000 BC. Roman soldiers sucked the leaves when they were thirsty and their doctors used it for their patients as a diuretic and also to cure scurvy.

The Tudors loved sorrel and ate it regularly to offset rich food. It is named after the old French word *surele*, which means sour. And it is still grown in most French kitchen gardens and sold in their food markets. In the rest of the world, unfortunately, it can be hard to find on sale, which is the very best reason to grow your own.

COOKING

Sorrel leaves are full of vitamin C and really lift a mixed leaf salad because of their lively, lemony taste and attractive shape. They contain vitamins A and C, as well as oxalic acid, which provides the tart taste. I pick small, young leaves of all three types of sorrel to eat raw. But I also use the more mature, large leaves of broad-leaf sorrel for wrapping around fish and other food.

One special appetizer is to make parcels of white crab meat in large sorrel leaves, steam for about 4 minutes and serve on a bed of sauce made from the brown crab meat, lemon juice and cream. A far simpler option is to make an omelette with a wilted sorrel filling. Eggs and the sharpness of sorrel go very well together. I also make quiche with chopped sorrel and strips of smoked salmon as the base. And the Sorrel and Sweetbread Terrine on page 160 is a favourite in our household. I cook sorrel in butter to make a purée, which I freeze for using later in soups and sauces.

Pick and wash sorrel leaves just before you want to use them because they soon begin to wilt. Large sorrel leaves are usually shredded before cooking, using the technique *en chiffonade*. This method of cutting large herb leaves – like broad-leaf sorrel, mint or basil – into fine shreds for sauces or for decorating salads or other recipes is a traditional culinary technique. You wash the leaves, discard the stems and pile up several leaves on top of one another. You then roll them up tightly until they resemble a cigar.

Secure the cigar with one hand, keeping your fingers tucked in. Then, using a very sharp knife, slice the roll of leaves very thinly to make shreds. With sorrel, these shreds dissolve quickly in a heated pan and are soon incorporated into a sauce. They also look interesting as raw, thin shreds, decorating the food on the plate that is being served with a sorrel sauce.

GROWING

All three types of sorrel are perennials, which are easy to look after. I collect the seeds in late summer when they have turned from green to red/brown. I sow some seeds soon after harvesting and others in early spring. Plants should be about 30cm/12in apart. They are less succulent if they grow too close together.

The most important thing with sorrel is to cut off the flower/seed stems regularly to keep the leaves growing well. Then you will always have fresh, tasty leaves for the kitchen. Sorrel is not fussy, growing in sun or partial shade, in pots, window boxes or in the ground. My plants are in leaf for most of the year and the more leaves you pick the better it grows. It is thought to prefer rich, acidic, damp soil, but mine thrives in our limestone area in light, often dry soil – the opposite conditions. I was not a fan of red-veined sorrel until I started to pick it very young and small, discovering these tender, pretty leaves do have taste as well as good looks.

SORREL

SORREL AND SWEETBREAD TERRINE

I discovered this recipe in Joyce Molyneux's book, *The Carved Angel Cookery Book*. It is full of brilliant dishes and her food at the restaurant of that name in Dartmouth was always wonderful too. It came as no surprise when she became one of the first women chefs to win a Michelin star. I once ate a meal at her restaurant all based on wild fungi collected locally that autumn. When I first met Simon Hopkinson, the chef behind the Bibendum restaurant and many excellent books, we both realized that Joyce Molyneux was our heroine and I rashly invited him for dinner the following evening. Rash, because it is always hard cooking for such a talented chef and also I was moving house the next day. I cooked him three of Joyce's recipes, including this special terrine. Over the years I have modified her recipe a little, but this is dedicated to her.

450g/1lb sweetbreads
350g/12oz belly of pork,
  chopped or minced/ground
2 handfuls of broad-leaf sorrel,
  leaves picked and chopped
2 eggs, lightly beaten
1 tbsp plain/all-purpose flour
freshly grated nutmeg
3–4 bay leaves
115g/4oz thin streaky green
  bacon slices, rinds removed
sea salt and freshly ground
  black pepper
Spiced Fruit (see page 167) and
  mixed salad with sorrel leaves,
  to serve

Prepare the sweetbreads by soaking them in cold water for 1–2 hours. Then bring them to the boil in fresh water and simmer for 10 minutes. Leave to cool in the cooking water. When they are cool, drain, remove any membranes and slice them into 4 or 5 sections.

Preheat the oven to 180°C/350°F/Gas 4. Mix the pork with the sorrel, eggs and flour and season with a good grating of nutmeg, salt and pepper.

Place 3–4 bay leaves down the length of a 1.2 litre/2 pint/5 cup terrine. Stretch the bacon by pulling it tightly across the back of a knife, then use it to line the terrine, leaving about 2.5cm/1in hanging over the top. Be careful that the bay leaves don't move too much under the bacon as they will be the decoration on top.

Spoon a layer of sorrel mix into the terrine, then a layer of sliced sweetbreads until the terrine is full. Make sure a sorrel mix layer is on the top. Flip over the bacon to seal in the filling. Stand the terrine in a roasting pan half-filled with hot water and cook in the oven for 2 hours until it is firm and has started to shrink from the sides of the terrine. Allow to cool. Serve with spiced fruit and salad, preferably small leaves of sorrel mixed with other salad leaves.

Preparation: 30 mins, plus soaking
Cooking: 2 hrs 10 mins

Serves 4

SORREL AND POTATO SALAD WITH SORREL SAUCE

This combination was served to 30 guests at a special birthday celebration recently and we often make it for up to 20 people at my herb courses. Everyone loves the sharp sorrel taste and the beauty of a plate of green food. We serve the sauce and salad with chicken or various types of fish, and it can also be used in a vegetarian dish by drizzling it over barbecued summer vegetables.

175/6oz small new potatoes
1 handful of small tender sorrel, preferably buckler-leaf sorrel, with its small leaves left intact
juice of 1 lemon
2 tbsp capers, drained and rinsed
120ml/4fl oz/½ cup olive oil
sea salt and freshly ground black pepper
cooked chicken or fish, to serve

SORREL SAUCE
2 large handfuls of broad-leaf sorrel
30g/1oz/2 tbsp butter
150ml/5fl oz/scant ⅔ cup double/heavy cream
4 tbsp vegetable stock
3 tbsp dry Vermouth or dry white wine

Cook the potatoes in a pan of boiling water, then drain and leave to cool.

Prepare the sorrel *en chiffonade*. Wash the leaves, discard the stems and pile up several leaves on top of one another. Roll them up tightly until they resemble a cigar, and secure with one hand, keeping your fingers tucked in. Using a very sharp knife, slice the roll of leaves very thinly to make shreds.

To make the sauce, melt the butter in a saucepan over a low heat and add the sorrel until it dissolves to a purée. Add the cream, stir in the stock and then the Vermouth or wine. Simmer for several minutes, season to taste and remove from the heat.

Just before serving, add the sorrel leaves, lemon juice, capers and oil to the potatoes, because sorrel can wilt if left in the dressing for too long.

Serve your chosen chicken or fish drizzled with the sauce and with the salad on the side.

Serves 4

Preparation: 20 mins
Cooking: 20 mins

SORREL FEAST OF BABY VEGETABLES AND STEAK

When your salad herbs are young and tasty, use a mix of sorrel with peppery leaves, like rocket/arugula, Greek cress, red mustards and chicory/Belgian endive, as a base for this delicious feast of steak and vegetables.

2 handfuls of broad-leaf sorrel

6 handfuls of a salad herb mix like rocket/arugula, red mustards, chicory/Belgian endive and Greek cress, or a bag of mixed leaves

12 small new potatoes

8 spears of asparagus

2 tbsp olive oil

2 beef sirloin steaks, about 175g/6oz each

6 young courgettes/zucchini, cut into 2.5cm/1in slices

55g/2oz Parmesan cheese, shaved

sea salt and freshly ground black pepper

ROSEMARY SALAD DRESSING

2 garlic cloves, crushed

1 tbsp finely chopped young rosemary leaves

zest and juice of 1 lemon

4 tbsp extra virgin olive oil

HORSERADISH CREAM

1 tbsp double/heavy cream

2 tbsp horseradish sauce

Preparation: 20 mins
Cooking: 20 mins

Remove the thick stalks of the sorrel and tear the leaves into smaller pieces. Arrange on a large serving plate with the salad herbs and leave to one side.

Mix together all the ingredients for the salad dressing and season with salt and pepper. Mix together the cream and horseradish sauce.

Cook the new potatoes in boiling water for about 15 minutes until tender, then drain. Once they have been cooking for 10 minutes, cook the asparagus in a separate pan of boiling water for about 5 minutes until tender, then drain.

Meanwhile, heat a griddle pan over a medium heat, add half the oil. Season the steaks and cook for about 6 minutes on each side. Remove from the pan and slice thinly. Add the remaining oil to the pan and fry the courgettes/zucchini for 5 minutes, or until browned on both sides but still slightly crisp.

Drizzle a little of the dressing over the salad. Arrange the warm vegetables, thin slices of steak and the Parmesan shavings on top and serve with the horseradish sauce and the remaining dressing on the side.

Serves 4

SORREL AND SALMON FISHCAKES

Most of the people I cook for regularly like fishcakes and I experiment with several fish and herb combinations. This recipe is a family favourite and I think the richness of salmon is improved by adding the sharp, lemon taste of the sorrel.

900g/2lb floury potatoes
750g/1lb 10oz salmon steaks
600ml/21fl oz/2½ cups fish
  stock
250g/9oz sorrel, leaves picked
  and finely chopped
a little plain/all-purpose flour,
  for dusting
2 eggs, beaten
140g/5oz/2½ cups brown
  breadcrumbs
3 tbsp olive oil, for frying
sea salt and freshly ground
  black pepper
crisp mixed salad herbs
  including raw sorrel, to serve

Cook the potatoes in boiling water until tender, which will take about 20 minutes. Drain and mash.

Meanwhile, put the salmon steaks in a saucepan, add the stock and simmer for 12 minutes until the fish flakes easily when tested with a fork. Leave to cool, then break into small flakes.

Warm the prepared sorrel in a large pan over a medium heat for 1 minute to soften.

Mix the salmon, potatoes and sorrel together and season with salt and pepper. Shape into fish cakes of the size you like. Cover with cling film/plastic wrap and chill for 20 minutes. Dip each fishcake into a little flour, then into the beaten eggs and then press the breadcrumbs on well.

Heat the oil in a frying pan and fry the fish cakes over a medium heat for 5 minutes each side until piping hot throughout and crisp on outside. Serve with a crisp mixed salad made of salad herbs, including raw sorrel.

Serves 4

Preparation: 30 mins, plus chilling
Cooking: 30 mins

HERB PRESERVES

I make a lot of preserves: for myself, to give as presents and to sell for charity. We have a mixed orchard and a lot of soft fruit, so it is a vital way to conserve any of the harvest that I cannot give away! During the winter months we enjoy the tastes of summer and autumn through preserves, which give something extra to our food. There are a few rules to follow. Homemade preserves are often made with vinegar, so are less susceptible to bacterial infections like botulism. But always use sterilized jars: wash, rinse, then put upside down in an oven heated to 110°C/225°F/Gas ½ for 30 minutes, and fill and seal while still hot. If the jar lids are old, line them with parchment paper. Choose good-quality, unblemished fruit and vegetables.

APPLE AND HERB JELLY

When the apple trees in our orchard are groaning under the weight of their fruits, I make jars of apple and herb jelly using a variety of herbs, including mint, sage, tarragon, marjoram, lavender, rosemary, lemon thyme, scented geraniums, rose petals and also a few jars spiced with chilli, peppercorns and bay. The apples can be windfalls, crab apples, cookers or sharp eating apples. The mint jelly is good with lamb and I often glaze the meat with it before cooking. The sage jelly is used in the same way with pork, while chilli jelly is particularly useful as a glaze.

2kg/4lb 8oz apples, washed, peeled, cored
  and quartered
juice of 2 lemons
granulated sugar (see method)
2 handfuls of your chosen herb, plus extra for
  identifying the jelly in the jar

Cook the apples in the lemon juice and 1.2litres/40fl oz/ 5 cups of water for 30 minutes until reduced to a pulp. Put the pulp into a jelly bag and leave to drip overnight.

Measure the juice into a pan and add 450g/1lb sugar and 2 handfuls of the herb for each 500ml/17fl oz/generous 2 cups juice. Stir over a gentle heat until the sugar dissolves, then boil hard for about 10 minutes. Skim, sieve to remove the cooked herbs, then pour into the sterilized jars (see above) and add a sprig of herb or 1 tbsp chopped herb to each jar.

Makes about 900g/2lb
Preparation: 50 mins, plus overnight draining
Cooking: 45 mins

POACHED PLUM AND LEMON VERBENA SAUCE

This is a marvellous lemony plum sauce, which can be used with puddings or made into a savoury, fruit sauce for dishes like pork or roast duck.

400g/14oz plums, pitted
1 large sprig of lemon verbena (about 40 leaves)
about 175g/6oz/1 cup sugar, to taste (you
  shouldn't need to add more than this)

Put the plums in a saucepan with a tiny splash of water – just enough to stop them sticking. Add the lemon verbena and sugar and simmer the plums until they are breaking down. This might take up to about 30 minutes, depending on how ripe they are. Sieve to leave a smooth sauce and transfer to a sterilized jar whilst still warm.

Makes about 500g/1lb 2oz
Preparation: 15 mins
Cooking: 30 mins

SPICED FRUIT WITH HERBS

I spice plums, damsons, crab apples, cherries, pears and even apple, using hard herbs like bay, rosemary, sage, savory or thyme. Good with pâtés, hams and cheeses.

400g/14oz/2 cups sugar
350ml/12fl oz/1½ cups white wine vinegar
5cm/2in cinnamon stick, broken into pieces
8 peppercorns
2.5cm/1in piece of root ginger, sliced
3 red dried chillies
4 bay leaves
1 large sprig of sage, savory, rosemary or thyme
1.3kg/3lb prepared fruit

Simmer all the ingredients apart from the fruit in a heavy pan for about 10 minutes, so the sugar dissolves and the flavours develop. Then put in the fruit and cook until tender. This may take only 2 minutes for small fruits like crab apples or up to 10 minutes for larger fruit like pears. Pack into warm sterilized jars (see opposite) and store for up to a year. The spicy taste increases over time.

Makes about 2kg/5lb
Preparation: 25 mins
Cooking: 20 mins

COURGETTE, ROSEMARY, GINGER AND CARDAMOM PRESERVE

This is excellent served with cheese, pâté, cold meats and grilled/broiled vegetables.

1.8kg/4lb courgettes/zucchini or marrow
900g/2lb/4½ cups sugar
zest and juice of 2 lemons
4 pieces of preserved ginger, chopped
1 handful of young rosemary leaves, finely chopped
12 green cardamom pods

Remove the seeds from the courgettes/zucchini, then chop the flesh into small cubes and simmer in boiling water for about 3 minutes. Drain well. Mix in the sugar and leave overnight. Then put in a pan with the remaining ingredients and simmer gently until the sugar dissolves. Bring to the boil, then simmer gently for 10–15 minutes until the vegetable is translucent and the syrup thick. Store in sterilized jars (see opposite).

Makes about 2kg/5lb
Preparation: 22 mins, plus overnight macerating
Cooking: 20 mins

[WHY NOT TRY...]

+ Making tarts with Apple and Herb Jelly spread over sliced fruit on a puff pastry base (see page 129)
+ Adding Spiced Fruit with Herbs to a cheeseboard or charcuterie platter, or using it as a topping for a whole melting, baked Camembert
+ Using Courgette and Rosemary Preserve in place of chutney in a sandwich or ploughman's lunch
+ Spreading Apple and Herb Jelly on a slice of buttered toast

WINTER

WINTER HERBS

Herbs are vital during the winter months to add depth to dishes like roasted vegetables, risotto, soups and casseroles and to generally cheer up the palate. It is amazing how many herbs will grow through the coldest weather, even the finer herbs like chervil, parsley and salad burnet. It is always reassuring to know that when hardy species, like rosemary, sage and bay, are picked and used in the kitchen during these winter months, they will bring life to heavier recipes with their aroma and strong flavour.

But these herbs are also vital to the look of my herb garden during the winter months. I use various sages, with their strong shapes, to highlight paths and formal beds. My thymes look good throughout the year and the long hedges of clipped herbs are invaluable. I also use salad burnet, violets, sorrel, wall germander, alpine strawberries, primroses, flatleaf and curly parsleys and par-cel to edge beds because they all look attractive during the winter.

I prune the sages after flowering, which always results in lots of new, fresh growth. So by late autumn I am cutting bunches to dry and hang in the kitchen. I like the look and smell of them and they are used on miserable, wet evenings when I do not feel like venturing out to cut fresh leaves. I also cut bay to hang in the kitchen for the same reasons. But rosemary is always used fresh.

I cut back other herbs before the winter months, so that the fresh leaves of chives, lemon balm, marjoram and angelica, for example, are free to push through the soil when warmer weather returns. The thymes are cut back straight after flowering, and then used for taking cuttings and drying in the kitchen, but I leave the seed heads on hyssop so that I can collect them in perfect condition for sowing in trays in the greenhouse. Every year I grow white, blue and pink hyssop from seed. They fill the herb beds and are now being planted in pots and borders for late flower colour in other parts of the garden, too.

The large, white seed heads of garlic chives are left on to dry and look attractive throughout the winter. I grow them in six clumps in a circle around the Apothecary's Rose which sits in the middle of my formal beds. After all the cutting back, I weed and clear the beds, make sure that the thymes have plenty of grit around their roots to help drainage and survival, and add homemade compost to the herbs that need nourishment, like lovage and salad herbs.

In the bed where I grow these winter salad herbs – which this year includes rocket/arugula, wild rocket/ arugula, Greek cress, French sorrel, buckler-leaf sorrel, red-veined sorrel, mibuna, mizuna, lamb's lettuce/corn salad, claytonia, namenia, mustards, coriander/cilantro, endives and chicories – I get as much compost down as possible and if there are any spaces I lay down black plastic to warm the soil ready for the growing season. I am now also having to net these herbs when pigeons become a pest, and use fleece in the coldest weeks.

I sow seeds in small trays to have parsley, dill and salad herbs as micro-herbs during the winter and also enjoy eating salad burnet with more traditional leaves like lettuce. The mild cucumber taste is not stunning, but the attractive shape of the leaves looks great on the plate. But the star herb of winter months for me is chervil. It grows happily and is used daily in many recipes, often as a substitute for tarragon when that is still underground. I make chervil sauces (see page 191), Smoked Salmon and Chervil Pâté (see page 190) and wonderful chervil tarts. It is an excellent addition to mayonnaise served with seafood and to plain omelettes. The leaf shape is so exquisite that when I make a pâté or cheese including the herb I always decorate the pot of food with whole leaves spread out on top and pressed into the surface.

Delicate herbs like this are always added at the end of cooking, unlike the hard herbs which are put in at the start of preparing dishes so that they infuse their taste thoroughly. Resinous, perfumed rosemary is great in Pumpkin, Chorizo and Rosemary Risotto (see page 186), Apple and Herb Jelly (see page 166), roast potatoes, white beans and chorizo, kebabs, with pear dishes and, of course, with lamb.

Bay is used for anything from flavouring a Bolognese sauce to finishing off complex pâtés, like the Sorrel and Sweetbread Terrine on page 160. Along with oregano, bay is one of the classic herb flavourings in Greek Lamb Kleftiko (see page 180) – a hearty roast for chilly winter days. It also works in sweet dishes. For special occasions I make my popular Bay Ice Cream (see page 111) or Bay-Infused Crème Brûlée, often served to a large group with my Party Fruit in Port (see page 182).

[WINTER ACTION LIST]

+ Sow seeds that need very low temperatures to germinate. Included in those species which depend on a period of "stratification", are sweet woodruff, cowslip, violet and sweet cicely. Sow in trays, cover with glass and leave outside in the cold.

+ Finish cutting back all the herbs, collecting any seeds left on them for sowing in the spring. If it is not too cold, divide perennial herbs and give the plants away to inspire friends and neighbours to start a herb bed.

+ Spread compost and use fleece to warm any tender plants. Keep the salad herbs weed free and protect from hungry birds.

+ When half-hardy herbs in pots are taken inside, prune them all and cut back on watering as they will be going into a dormant state.

+ Cut back, dry and hang bunches of bay and winter savory in the kitchen. I tie large bunches of bay in glossy red ribbon to give to friends at Christmas with a label saying "Happy Christmas Bay"! Some friends leave the bay bunch up all year in the kitchen to provide dried bay for cooking, after tying it to their front doors to make a welcome Christmas statement. I make a more complicated wreath for my own front door with bay, rosemary, dried orange slices, red chillies and clementines.

+ In late winter, I start some seeds in the greenhouse, including basil, parsley and tomatoes. Begin to water the pots of half-hardy herbs like scented geraniums and lemon verbena and watch them start to come to life. While snowdrops and hellebores are lighting up the flower borders, tiny shoots of chives are pushing through the soil, reminding me that the herbs hibernating under the ground will soon be inspiring my cooking.

BAY

No cook should be without bay leaves. They are an essential seasoning, like sea salt and freshly ground black pepper, enhancing a dish with their deep, rich, resinous flavour, which has a hint of lemons and almonds. I use them every day, so I was thrilled to find our small farm had a huge bay tree when we moved here over 20 years ago. So it is easy for me to always have a small jug of fresh bay leaves by the cooker, as well as a bunch of dried leaves hanging in the kitchen. My family and friends all have my bay bunches by their cooking areas, too.

HISTORY

Bay, *Laurus nobilis*, originated in Asia Minor, soon spread to the Mediterranean and is now grown around the world. *Laurus* means praise and *nobilis* famous. So the Ancient Romans, who had great respect for this herb, crowned athletes with a bay wreath to reward their success, while poets were crowned with the same herb to celebrate their wisdom. Hence the title – Poet Laureate.

COOKING

When you are using bay, remember that fresh leaves have a stronger flavour than dried. The superb taste is unlocked by heat, often in a liquid when soups, stews and stocks/broths are being prepared. But bay is just as wonderful in sweet dishes. I infuse a few fresh leaves in the hot base for ice cream or brûlée, or I heat them up with alcohol and dried fruits for a celebration compôte.

I use bay in terrines, marinades, conserves, milk custards, rice puddings, cheese sauces, béchamel, Indian recipes, with poached fruit, fish and chicken as well as tomato dishes, like Italian pasta sauces. I often slip bay leaves between cubes of meat, vegetables or prawns/shrimp on a skewer, after soaking the skewers in warm water for an hour or so to make them more resistant to burning. As the leaves heat up under the grill/broiler or on the barbecue, the aroma of the bay improves the flavour of the main ingredients. Do not worry about using too many bay leaves in this way, because you never eat the tough leaves themselves, they are used just to impart their deep, rich flavour.

Bay is an essential part of bouquet garni, used normally with thyme and parsley stalks, but oregano, rosemary, sage or savory can be added, too. Cut the herbs you are using into large sprigs and either tie together with cotton string or put them in a muslin/cheesecloth bag, perhaps with some peppercorns. Tie up tightly and use to flavour soups and stews.

I also add fresh leaves to jars of rice or sugar. And I make a spicy herb oil with bay, dried chilli and often other hard herbs. It is left in a dark place as the herbs release their flavours into extra virgin olive oil (see page 146). This has become a popular present for friends because they like to drizzle it over salads and other dishes for instant oomph. Dried bay bunches are a popular gift, too. Hang branches of fresh bay in a dark, airy place until they become brittle. The darkness is important to retain the green colour and flavour of the leaves. You can keep them in bunches, but the flavour will last longer if you strip off the leaves and store in an airtight container.

GROWING

A pair of standard bay trees, clipped into perfect spheres, in pots placed either side of a door or gate are a classic sight. It makes a lot of sense to grow bay in containers because they can be positioned in a warm, sheltered place and brought inside during the coldest, wettest months. Bay is prone to frost damage because it is shallow rooted and the leaves can also be scorched by low temperatures and cold winds. But whether you want to grow bay in pots or garden beds, it needs rich, well-drained soil, mulched in spring.

I take bay cuttings in late summer, but success rates are low, even using a heated propagator with high humidity. Bay can also be grown from seed, found in the berries on mature plants, but these normally take months to germinate. So the best idea, unless you are very patient, is to buy a small plant and enjoy using its leaves as you watch it grow over the years.

PEARS POACHED IN BAY AND BALSAMIC WITH SERRANO HAM

Poached pears wrapped in Serrano ham and served on a bed of attractive salad herb leaves makes a stunning first course. You can poach the pears a day or so in advance. Keep them in the refrigerator, but always serve the pears at room temperature to enhance their flavour.

200g/7oz/1 cup caster/
   superfine sugar
80ml/2½fl oz/⅓ cup balsamic
   vinegar
4 bay leaves
4 pears
4 large slices of Serrano ham
2 large handfuls of multi-
   coloured salad herbs, such
   as rocket/arugula, cress, red
   mustard or lamb's lettuce/
   corn salad
3 tbsp pine nuts, toasted
1 tbsp olive oil
sea salt and freshly ground
   black pepper

Put 600ml/21fl oz/2½ cups of water in a saucepan over a medium heat with the sugar, vinegar and bay leaves. Bring to the boil, then simmer until the sugar has dissolved.

Peel the pears, leaving the stalks intact. Trim the bases so that they can stand upright. Add the pears to the liquid and simmer until they are tender, turning occasionally. The time varies a great deal depending on how ripe they are, but it should be 10–25 minutes. Remove the pears from the liquid and allow to cool, then wrap each one in a slice of ham.

Season the liquid, using only a little salt because of the ham in this recipe, but be generous with the freshly ground black pepper. Boil the liquid until it becomes a thick syrup.

Arrange the salad leaves on serving plates. Put a pear in the middle of each and scatter the pine nuts around the pears. Mix the balsamic syrup with the oil and drizzle over the top.

Serves 4

Preparation: 30 mins
Cooking: 35 mins

GUINEA FOWL WITH BAY LENTILS AND BACON

This dish relies a lot on the flavour of bay and the lentils, which are cooked with this herb. The recipe for preparing the lentils and other serving ideas based on these herby lentils are on the opposite page.

2 bay leaves
1 large guinea fowl
1 tbsp olive oil
4 whole unpeeled garlic cloves
175g/6oz smoked bacon
  lardons/diced thick-sliced
  smoked bacon
12 small shallots
185ml/6fl oz/¾ cup
  chicken stock
1 tbsp redcurrant jelly
175g/6oz/2 cups prepared Bay
  Lentils (see opposite)
sea salt and freshly ground
  black pepper

Preheat the oven to 220°C/425°F/Gas 7. Stuff the bay leaves into the cavity of the guinea fowl, rub with oil, season with salt and pepper and place breast-side down in a roasting pan. Cook for 30 minutes, then turn the bird, putting extra pepper on the breasts and legs. Add the whole garlic cloves, the bacon and the peeled shallots to the pan. Cook them in the juices around the guinea fowl for about 20 minutes until the bird is cooked through and nicely browned.

When it is ready, take the guinea fowl out of the pan and transfer to an ovenproof dish. Lift out the other ingredients with a slotted spoon and put them on the dish with the guinea fowl to keep warm in the bottom of the turned-off oven. Add the chicken stock and redcurrant jelly to the juices and simmer until the sauce has the consistency of double/heavy cream, stirring to mix in all the cooking juices.

Meanwhile, heat through the lentils in a separate saucepan, then spoon them onto the same dish around the guinea fowl with the lardons, shallots and garlic arranged on top. Serve with the sauce on the side.

Serves 4

Preparation: 20 mins
Cooking: 1 hr

BAY LENTILS

Bay-flavoured lentils are one of many standbys I like to keep in the refrigerator after a marathon cooking session. The secret is to flavour well and never overcook. Simmer them for only 20 minutes, when they will be cooked but still have a bite. Sludgy, tasteless lentils are not worth eating and have harmed the reputation of these earthy pulses/legumes. We have just had lunch as I write this recipe, made up of baked peppers and mushrooms baked with mozzarella, served on a bed of these marvellous bay lentils.

1 large onion, quartered
2 celery stalks, halved
2 carrots, halved or quartered
1 red chilli
2 garlic cloves
6 bay leaves
500g/1lb 2oz/2¾ cups Puy lentils, rinsed
3 tbsp sherry vinegar
2 tbsp olive oil

Put the vegetables, chilli, garlic and bay leaves in the bottom of a large saucepan and add the lentils. Cover with water, bring to the boil, part-cover and simmer for 20 minutes. Drain and remove the vegetables. While the lentils are still warm, stir in the vinegar and oil. This means the lentils absorb their flavours better.

Quantity for 3–4 recipes

Preparation: 15 mins
Cooking: 25 mins

VARIATIONS

LENTILS WITH GOATS' CHEESE AND AVOCADO

When the lentils are still hot, you can wilt sorrel leaves or spinach through them, add a little lemon juice and serve with goats' cheese portions and sliced avocado.

LENTILS WITH SMOKED MACKEREL, BACON AND HERBS

Mix the bay lentils with chopped herbs like thyme or coriander/cilantro. Serve with cold slices of mackerel and warm bacon lardons.

LENTILS WITH ROAST CHICKEN AND AIOLI

Roast a chicken and several tomatoes. Make a herb oil with chervil or basil (see page 146) and prepare some aioli by adding a very finely chopped garlic clove to your mayonnaise (see Chive Mayonnaise on page 32). On a bed of warm lentils, serve the warm chicken and tomatoes, pour over the herb oil and serve with the aioli.

LUSCIOUS LENTIL SOUP

Cumin is perfect in a soup made from lentils. If you have plenty of Bay Lentils left, add a can of chopped/crushed tomatoes, vegetables like carrots, courgettes/zucchini and onions and ground cumin to taste. Blitz it up with some good-quality stock, then warm through in a saucepan before serving.

ASIAN LENTILS

When you cook the bay lentils, instead of using sherry vinegar and olive oil, you can mix them with soy sauce and sesame oil, ready to serve them with your favourite Asian recipes for chicken or fish.

LAMB KLEFTIKO

6 garlic cloves, chopped

3 tbsp dried oregano

grated zest and juice of 1 lemon

a pinch of ground cinnamon

4 tbsp olive oil

1 large leg of lamb, at least
  2kg/4lb 8oz

1kg/2lb 4oz new potatoes,
  halved

4 bay leaves

sea salt and freshly ground
  black pepper

GREEK SALAD

½ cucumber, diced

3 large vine tomatoes, diced

¼ red onion, sliced

12 black pitted Kalamata
  olives

60g/2¼oz feta cheese, diced

3 tbsp extra virgin olive oil

dried oregano, to sprinkle

MINT YOGURT

250g/9oz/generous 1 cup
  Greek yogurt

juice of ½ lemon

1 tbsp olive oil

1 handful of mint, leaves picked
  and chopped

Kleftiko means stolen. Apparently lambs were taken from Greek farmers by Klephts centuries ago, who cooked the animals in pits in the ground to hide the smell of cooking so they didn't get caught. It also sealed in the flavour so cooking lamb *kleftiko* underground continued for many years because the results were so delicious. I first tasted the dish in Cyprus in 1975, the year after the Turkish invasion. My husband had been there during the war the year before, working for the BBC. He loved the island so much that we went on to have many holidays there in a house by a beach called Coral Bay, which had one restaurant, owned by the Charalambous family. Their kleftiko was delicious. It is a good recipe for feeding hoards of people so we also ate it at weddings of members of local families we got to know.

Crush the garlic, oregano, lemon zest and juice, cinnamon and oil to make a paste. Make slits in the lamb with the tip of a sharp knife and rub in the paste, pushing it into the slits, and season with salt and pepper. Cover with a food bag or cling film/plastic wrap, and leave in the refrigerator to marinate overnight.

Remove the lamb from the refrigerator a good hour before you want to cook it so that it returns to room temperature. Preheat the oven to 160°C/315°F/Gas 2–3.

In a large casserole dish, put in the potatoes and bay leaves, and place the lamb on top. Cover with parchment paper and then the lid and put in the oven for up to 4 hours until the meat is very tender. Take off the lid and paper and baste the lamb with the juices. Turn the heat up to 220°C/425°F/Gas 7 and return the lamb to the oven for about 30 minutes until browned.

Make the Greek salad by tossing together all the ingredients. Transfer to a serving bowl and sprinkle over the dried oregano. Stir together the ingredients for the mint yogurt.

Serve the lamb and potatoes with the mint yogurt and Greek salad.

Serves 8

Preparation: 30 mins, plus marinating
Cooking: 4–5 hrs

BAY-INFUSED CRÈME BRÛLÉE

This delicious dessert starts in the same way as the Bay Ice Cream (see page 111). You make the bay custard in the same way as you would for an ice cream, but instead of freezing, set the custard in the oven instead.

1 recipe quantity Basic Ice Cream (see page 110)
4 tsp caster/superfine sugar

Follow the recipe to make bay infused custard, as on pages 110–11. When you get to the point the custard is ready to go into the ice cream maker, stop and preheat the oven to 180°C/350°F/Gas 4 instead.

Pour the custard into individual ramekins/custard cups and put them in a roasting pan. Pour in hot water to come half-way up the sides of the ramekins. Bake until the mixture is just set, about 30–40 minutes. Remove from the oven and leave to cool.

Just before serving, sprinkle a teaspoon of sugar on the top of each custard and put them under a very hot grill/broiler until the sugar turns deep brown and crisp. You can use a blowtorch to caramelize them instead, if you have one.

Serves 4

Preparation: 15 mins, plus infusing
Cooking: 40 mins

BAY PARTY FRUIT IN PORT

This is a festive dish to serve with Bay Ice Cream (see page 111) or Bay-Infused Crème Brûlée (left). It is good for a party because it can be made ahead and stored in the refrigerator for three days, where the flavour improves by the day. It is especially good served with preserved clementines, which you can make by poaching clementines for 12 minutes in enough water to cover with 1 teaspoon ground cinnamon, 3 tablespoons sugar and 2 bay leaves. Decant into warm sterilized jars (see page 166) and pour over a mixture of the poaching syrup with 1 tablespoon cooking brandy to each jar. Wait at least two weeks before using.

450g/1lb/3 cups dried fruit of your choice, such
   as dried apricots, dried Agen prunes, dried pears
   or dates
4 bay leaves
grated zest and juice of 1 orange
250ml/9fl oz/generous 1 cup port
50g/1¾oz/scant ⅔ cup flaked/sliced almonds,
   toasted

First soak the dried fruit in water to remove any preservatives. Rinse again in water and put in a pan with the bay leaves and enough water to just cover. Simmer until the fruit is tender, which will take 15–20 minutes. Add the orange zest and juice and the port. Cool and chill, then keep in a refrigerator for at least 2 days for the flavours to develop. Serve sprinkled with the toasted almonds.

Serves 8
Preparation: 15 mins, plus chilling
Cooking: 20 mins

RISOTTO

There is an Italian saying that "rice is born in water, but it must die in wine", which is a good excuse for drinking wine when eating or even cooking this dish. Risotto has been part of the Italian diet since the 8th century when Arabs introduced rice to Sicily. So they should know. As these quotes show – "making risotto is like making love – you have to be totally involved with the process"; "when stock is first added to the dish, you will be rewarded by a sigh"; "stir and caress it into a velvet-smooth masterpiece" – chefs can be a little pretentious about this dish.

There is a lot of disagreement about the perfect rice to use for risotto and the perfect technique. Arborio rice is popular and easy to find, but its large grains need to be cooked carefully and taken off the heat to rest before they are fully cooked. I like the excellent Carnaroli for important recipes, like the saffron Risotto alla Milanese I often serve for special meals (see page 140). It is the least likely to overcook and become mushy. Apparently it contains a substance that helps the grains to keep their texture and shape. Always use a wooden spoon and a pan with a rounded base so there are no corners where the rice can stick.

I first tried to cook risotto on a single gas ring when I was a student at Durham University in the 1960s. This was on the glamorous Norman Gallery in Durham Castle, where my boyfriend was lucky enough to have rooms. I had no cooking skills at all and he never knew that I took off one of my stockings to sieve the sloppy rice before I added the prawns/shrimp. It was a disaster, which may be one reason why he likes cooking risotto today, never leaving the stove as he stirs towards creamy perfection. He likes trying new ideas, so I bought him a book recently which contains 85 recipes – all for risotto!

BASIC RISOTTO

l large onion, chopped
2 celery stalks, finely chopped
1 tbsp olive oil
50g/1¾oz/3½ tbsp butter
2 garlic cloves, finely chopped
300g/10½oz/1⅔ cups risotto rice
about 300ml/10½fl oz/1¼ cups dry white wine
1 litre/35fl oz/4⅓ cups hot stock to match recipe
50g/1¾oz Parmesan cheese, grated
sea salt and freshly ground black pepper

Gently fry the onion and celery in the oil and half the butter until just beginning to soften, then add the garlic and cook for 2 minutes. Turn up the heat, add the rice and stir until it becomes opaque. Add the wine and cook for a few minutes to evaporate the alcohol. Add the stock one ladle at a time, stirring to release the starch and give a creamy texture but maintaining grains that are firm to the bite. Take off the heat, stir in the cheese, seasoning and remaining butter. Cover and rest for 20–25 minutes. This stage, *mantecare*, makes the risotto even more creamy.

Serves 4   Preparation: 15 mins, plus resting   Cook: 25 mins

RISOTTO

PUMPKIN, CHORIZO AND ROSEMARY RISOTTO

This is a gutsy recipe with great colour provided by the pumpkin and a powerful taste from the combination of rosemary and chorizo.

450g/1lb pumpkin or squash, skinned, deseeded and cut into small pieces
1 recipe quantity Basic Risotto using vegetable stock (see page 184)
100–175g/3½–6oz raw chorizo (depending on how strong you like it), finely chopped
2 tbsp finely chopped rosemary leaves

Bring a large pan of water to the boil, add the pumpkin and cook for 5 minutes, or until just beginning to soften. Drain thoroughly.

Make the risotto, following the instructions on page 184, until the wine has evaporated. Add the chorizo and cook for 3 minutes before adding the pumpkin pieces. Stir in half the rosemary. Continue with the recipe, gradually adding the stock, one ladle at a time and stirring constantly, for about 15 minutes. Season and add the remaining rosemary and butter and about half the Parmesan. Cover and leave to rest until creamy. Serve with the remaining Parmesan.

RISI E BISI

As soon as I left my student days behind I decided to learn how to cook. I was, after all, planning to eat for the rest of my life and I wanted to eat well. Courses were out of the question as I had to work, so I cooked my way through all of Elizabeth David's inspiring books and Risi e Bisi was the first Italian recipe I tried. I use more ham and fewer peas in my version and the parsley is an important addition, lifting the taste with its green, leafy freshness. It is best made with fresh peas, but if you want to serve it throughout the year, you will have to use frozen most of the time. Most people do, as it is rare to see people podding peas these days.

1 recipe quantity Basic Risotto using vegetable stock (see page 184)
225g/8oz uncooked gammon, finely chopped
1 onion, finely chopped
280g/10oz/heaped 2 cups fresh podded peas
2 tbsp finely chopped parsley leaves

Make the risotto following the instructions on page 184, frying the gammon and additional onion with the onion and celery. Continue with the recipe, gradually adding the stock, one ladle at a time, and stirring constantly. After 10 minutes, add the peas and parsley and season with salt and pepper. Continue to the end of the recipe but stir less frequently to avoid breaking up the peas. Risi e bisi is meant to be more liquid than normal risotto, but as it should be eaten with a fork, it must not be too soupy.

SEAFOOD RISOTTO WITH SWEET CICELY

The ingredients for this typically Venetian dish can vary depending on what your fishmonger has on offer and I often make it just with prawns/shrimp if that is all I have in the house. But you can be extravagant and use scallops, cooked mussels and even cooked lobster with the prawns/shrimp. Do not use Parmesan in fish recipes.

1 recipe quantity Basic Risotto, using fish stock (see page 184) and omitting the Parmesan
300g/10½oz tomatoes, skinned, deseeded and chopped (see page 24)
500g/1lb 2oz raw mixed seafood
4 tbsp chopped sweet cicely
2 bay leaves

Make the risotto following the instructions on page 184, adding the tomatoes with the garlic. Continue with the recipe to the end, adding the raw seafood, sweet cicely and bay leaves 5 minutes before the rice will be ready, when the seafood should have turned pink. If you are using cooked fish, stir it in just before leaving the risotto to rest.

RISOTTO

CHERVIL

Chervil is easy to grow as a hardy annual throughout the year, but is very hard to find on sale in food shops. In many ways it is my most important herb in the garden because it thrives in the cold winter months when so many other herbs disappear underground. Its beautiful, delicate, lacy leaves survive snow and frost, cheering up my food with their looks and aniseed taste. Chervil is the most subtle of aniseed-flavoured herbs and when tarragon hides under the cold soil, I use chervil instead in all the traditional tarragon recipes like Béarnaise Sauce (see page 191) and Tangy Tarragon Chicken (see page 74).

HISTORY

Native to Russia and the Middle East, it is thought that the Romans first brought chervil to Britain. It was used in many different herbal concoctions, including one to aid digestion, another to lower high blood pressure, and yet another to do the opposite because it was used as a stimulant. And it was even added to vinegar to cure hiccups. It was traditionally eaten in large quantities during the Christian time of Lent, especially on Maundy Thursday. Gerard, the Elizabethan doctor and garden supervisor, wrote enthusiastically about chervil in his book *Herbal*. It is now far more popular in France than other countries, where it is one ingredient in the famous *fines herbes* mix, and can often be found growing wild.

COOKING

Chervil is so delicate that it should be added to dishes at the end of cooking to avoid loss of flavour. It is great added chopped to vegetables like leeks, artichokes or broad/fava beans, adds zest to green salads and works well with many fish, chicken and egg dishes. I blend smoked fish with lemon juice, crème fraîche and lots of chervil to make a simple pâté (see page 190). Tarts are another favourite and it is excellent in vegetable soups. A traditional potato and carrot soup is lifted by adding chervil just before serving, and cauliflower and chervil soup is a classic. Chervil sauce made with shallots, lemon zest and juice, cream and stock is good with fish, chicken or veal. The herb is perfect with many vegetables, like carrots, beans, and the Jerusalem artichoke recipes on page 192. Finely chopped, it is a great addition to salad leaves and to my herby lentil recipes on page 179. Apparently the 18th century philosopher Voltaire loved chopped chervil added to scrambled eggs. We always serve chervil with smoked salmon and scrambled eggs for brunch on Christmas Day. I could not cook happily without chervil's great beauty and taste.

GROWING

Chervil is very easy to grow, and is known to prefer light soil, some moisture and semi shade, although I find that it also grows in full sun in my garden, often reaching 60cm/24in tall. It has white flowers, which you can remove to encourage leaf formation. You can grow it between other garden plants, like vegetables, to provide some shade, because if it gets too much sun and too little water, it will flower too early so that leaves are lost.

When the flowers form, I do leave a few of them to go to seed and so have only bought one packet of chervil seeds during my long herb-growing years. I pick the seeds when they go black and immediately sow them against the north wall of my herb garden, and in a few other areas, too. Some seeds are also grown in a tray in the greenhouse, covered with vermiculite. Germination is very quick and because these plants have long tap roots they need to be potted on quickly into deep pots or planted outside 23cm/9in apart. I save some of the seeds to sow in early spring so I have a constant supply of chervil throughout the year. The seed loses its viability after about 12 months.

After sowing, chervil is ready to harvest within a few weeks. My chervil has never had diseases or pests, but if the plants do become infected by greenfly, wash them gently because the soft leaves are damaged easily.

This is one of the herbs which are hard to grow in a pot on your kitchen windowsill because the plants become leggy and the leaves lose their colour and flavour inside. Chervil is not suitable for drying, but can be frozen as a herb butter or chopped finely and put into ice cube trays with a little water. It is rich in vitamin C and iron, is versatile enough to be used in dozens of my favourite recipes and can also be infused to make a refreshing tea. A top five-star herb.

SMOKED SALMON AND CHERVIL PÂTÉ

This simple pâté can be made with salmon pieces, which are often sold more cheaply than slices. It makes a lovely canapé or an easy first course served with the Cucumber Pickle with Dill (see page 90). Chervil is a good herb with salmon, but dill or chives can also be used when they are in season. I often serve a slice of cucumber with smoked salmon and chive pâté on top, finished with a chive flower, when they are available.

115g/4oz smoked salmon
350g/12oz/1½ cups cream cheese
2 tbsp finely chopped chervil leaves
a large pinch of cayenne pepper
juice of ½ lemon

Blend together all the ingredients. No other seasoning is necessary.

Serves 4

Preparation: 15 mins

CHICKEN LIVER PÂTÉ WITH APPLE AND CHERVIL

This is a refreshing pâté which can be served as a canapé on croûtes or as a first course with Spiced Fruit (see page 167) and salad.

450g/1lb chicken livers
55g/2oz/¼ cup butter
2 tbsp cooking brandy
1 onion, chopped
1 garlic clove, finely chopped
2 sharp eating apples, peeled, cored and diced
1 handful of chervil, leaves picked and finely chopped, plus a small sprig to decorate
90g/3oz/generous ⅓ cup clarified butter, melted (see page 78)
sea salt and freshly ground black pepper

Wash the livers and remove the membranes and any green-tinged areas. Melt half the butter in a frying pan and cook the livers gently for 2–3 minutes until all the pink colour has disappeared. Deglaze the pan with the brandy, stirring to mix in anything stuck to the bottom of the pan.

Soften the onion, garlic and apples in the rest of the butter in a separate pan for 5 minutes, then add to the livers with the chervil and season with salt and pepper. Blend everything together until smooth, then press gently into a pâté dish. Seal the pâté with the clarified butter and garnish with a sprig of chervil.

Serves 4

Preparation: 20 mins
Cooking: 10 mins

SAUCE FINES HERBES

This traditional and exquisite sauce can be served with fish, chicken and roasted or grilled/broiled vegetables.

55g/2oz/¼ cup butter
1 tbsp plain/all-purpose flour
90ml/3fl oz/6 tbsp vegetable stock
4 tbsp double/heavy cream
4 tbsp vermouth
1 handful of chervil in the winter or tarragon in spring and summer, leaves picked and chopped
2 tbsp chopped flatleaf parsley
2 tbsp snipped chives
sea salt and freshly ground black pepper

Blend together the butter and flour in a small saucepan over a low heat. Add the stock, cream and vermouth and simmer gently for about 4 minutes, whisking continuously, until the sauce has the consistency of single/light cream. Add the herbs and season well.

Serves 4   Preparation: 10 mins   Cooking: 5 mins

LEMON SAUCE

This simple, creamy sauce is refreshing with grilled/broiled meats and many types of fish.

1 onion, chopped
1 tbsp butter
grated zest and juice of ½ lemon
240ml/8fl oz/1 cup double/heavy cream
2 egg yolks
3 tbsp finely chopped chervil leaves
sea salt and freshly ground black pepper

Soften the chopped onion in the butter for about 8 minutes, without allowing it to brown. Add the lemon zest and juice, cream and egg yolks and whisk the sauce as you heat it over a medium heat for 10–15 minutes until it thickens. Add the chervil and season to taste with salt and pepper.

Serves 4   Preparation: 10 mins   Cooking: 25 mins

BÉARNAISE SAUCE

In the winter, when tarragon will have escaped underground, you can use chervil instead in this classic recipe. Both herbs have a similar aniseed taste. This is served with steak and many other dishes including fish and eggs.

4 tbsp dry white wine
4 tbsp white wine vinegar
2 tsp finely chopped shallot
2 egg yolks
140g/5oz/scant ⅔ cup butter
2 tbsp chopped chervil or French tarragon
sea salt and freshly ground black pepper

Boil the wine, vinegar, shallot and a pinch of pepper together until the pan is almost dry. Add 1 tablespoon of water immediately and take off the heat. Whisk in the egg yolks, then add the butter bit by bit, whisking over a gentle heat for about 4 minutes until it thickens. Add the chopped herb, season with salt and pepper, and stir well.

Serves 4   Preparation: 10 mins   Cooking: 10 mins

JERUSALEM ARTICHOKES WITH CHERVIL, RED ONION AND BACON

Jerusalem artichokes are very useful peeled and cooked gently until they are still slightly crisp. They can be served cold with many salads and other dishes. This is a favourite of mine, served with bacon lardons, raw red onion and lots of chopped chervil in a good Mustard Dressing.

16 Jerusalem artichokes, peeled
1 small red onion, finely chopped
3 tbsp chopped chervil leaves, plus extra to
   decorate
4 tbsp Mustard Dressing (see page 221)
100g/3½oz bacon lardons
sea salt and freshly ground black pepper

Boil the artichokes for 5–10 minutes, checking constantly, until just tender but still quite crisp – they must not soften. Drain and slice the artichokes thinly. Mix with the red onion, chopped chervil and the mustard dressing.

Fry the bacon for a few minutes until cooked through and just beginning to brown, then add it to the artichokes. Finish with a little extra chopped chervil and season with salt and pepper.

Serves 4

Preparation: 15 mins
Cooking: 20 mins

JERUSALEM ARTICHOKES WITH CHERVIL AND AVOCADO

Crisp, firm artichoke slices contrast beautifully with the soft and creamy avocado. The walnuts in the dressing work well with the taste of artichokes. I use them together in other recipes like sauces and soups.

16 Jerusalem artichokes, peeled
2 shallots, finely chopped
3 ripe avocados, peeled and pitted
3 tbsp chopped chervil leaves

WALNUT DRESSING
1 tbsp walnut oil
4 tbsp non-scented oil like sunflower or
   groundnut/peanut oil
1 tbsp white wine vinegar
1 tbsp walnuts, crushed in a pestle and mortar
sea salt and freshly ground black pepper

Prepare the artichokes as described in the recipe on the left. Mix with the raw chopped shallots. Slice the avocados and arrange the vegetables on a serving dish.

Make the walnut dressing by whisking together all the ingredients and seasoning well.

Sprinkle the chervil over the artichokes and avocado, season with salt and pepper and pour the dressing over the top.

Serves 4

Preparation: 20 mins
Cooking: 10 mins

ROAST JOHN DORY WITH CHERVIL AND ALMOND BUTTER

This is a subtle fish recipe to make the most of chervil when it is at its wonderful, winter best. I like to use John Dory for this dish, which I first ate in a small coastal village in Corsica. In French it is called St Pierre, supposedly because it bears St Peter's thumbprints from the time he caught the fish for Jesus. The recipe can be made with other fish, like sea bream.

2 large, whole John Dory, prepared by the fishmonger
juice of 1 lemon, plus 1 lemon, cut into wedges
2 tbsp roughly chopped flatleaf parsley leaves
3 small sprigs of rosemary leaves
sea salt and freshly ground black pepper

CHERVIL AND ALMOND BUTTER
85g/3oz/heaped 1 cup flaked/ sliced almonds
85g/3oz/heaped ⅓ cup butter
1 handful of chervil, leaves picked and finely chopped
juice of ½ lemon

Preheat the oven to 200°C/400°F/Gas 6. Rinse the fish and pat dry, then score the fish several times on each side. Mix the lemon juice with the parsley and rosemary and push half into the cavity of each fish. Season with salt and pepper. Put the fish on a baking tray with the lemon wedges and roast in the oven for 12 minutes until firm to the touch but cooked through.

Meanwhile, to make the chervil and almond butter, toast the almonds in a non-stick saucepan over a low heat for about 5 minutes until they brown. Add the butter and let it melt. Take off the heat and stir in the chervil, lemon juice and almonds until well mixed. Spoon over the fish, arrange the lemon wedges on top and serve warm. Simple and delicious.

Serves 4

Preparation: 10 mins
Cooking: 12 mins

CORIANDER

Coriander, or cilantro, is one of the most widely used herbs around the world, loved for the robust flavour of its leaves and seeds. The sweet, citrus, astringent taste of the leaves goes well with powerful salad, yogurt, cheese, soup, noodle, stir-fry and sauce recipes from the Middle East, India, Thailand, China, Mexico and North Africa. Coriander seed is useful for embedding flavour into slow cooked recipes like curries. This versatile herb has a "love it or hate it" flavour because it is so strong. But its increasing sales prove that more and more cooks are learning to appreciate coriander/cilantro and rely on it in their kitchens.

HISTORY

The oldest archaeological discovery of the seeds of coriander/cilantro was in a tomb in Israel. Many people believe that the "manna" eaten by the children of Israel returning from slavery in Egypt, described in the Old Testament, was in fact the seeds of the coriander/cilantro herb. It is still eaten during Passover to remind Jewish people of that historic journey. The Romans brought the plant to Northern Europe, using it to preserve meat. By the Middle Ages it had a reputation as an aphrodisiac, being an important ingredient in love potions. It has taken time to become popular in food. In 1597 the herb expert John Gerard described it as a "stinking herbe". Few people would agree with him today.

COOKING

Coriander/cilantro leaves should be added to dishes just before serving because the herb loses flavour and goes slimy if cooked for too long. The fragrance and character of the leaves adds so much to the big tastes of ginger, garlic, spices and particularly chilli, in recipes from around the world. Pick the white flowers to use in salads or rice dishes; they taste of both the leaves and seeds, an aromatic and scented mix. The seeds have a stronger taste with a hint of orange, enhanced when you heat them in a dry pan, then grind them to add to a dish.

GROWING

Coriander/cilantro is an annual herb related to carrots, which grows to a height of 75cm/30in. In the summer, attractive clusters of small white flowers appear, followed by the seeds. The leaves of coriander/cilantro come in two forms. The lower broad leaves are the first to grow and with their strong taste they are the best for the kitchen. Then upper, finely cut leaves appear, which have a less attractive taste and a rather pungent scent.

These second leaves are a sign that the plant will soon be producing flowers and then seeds. In hot, dry conditions coriander/cilantro will go to seed more quickly. Two varieties that are recommended as slow to bolt are Leisure and Confetti. The secret with all coriander/cilantro seed is to sow little and often in early spring and autumn, but not in the hot, dry months.

Harvest the leaves for cooking when they are bright green in colour. When flowering starts the leaf flavour deteriorates. Pick the white flowers just before you plan to use them, once the whole cluster is in flower. I pick some of the seeds when they are green because they have an amazing fresh spice flavour. But most are left on the plant until they turn beige and will then store well. At this stage the smell of the seeds starts to change and become attractive. This is the time to harvest them. Tie a paper bag over the seedheads and hang in an airy, dry place for about two weeks. The seeds can then be separated and stored in an airtight jar for cooking, or sown in the garden to provide the next crop.

Few people know that the root is edible and delicious. Its earthy flavour is a mix of the leaf and seed. Roots should be finely chopped and added to soups, stews and curries. They are often used in Thai recipes.

As coriander/cilantro hates to be transplanted, sow the seeds directly into garden soil where you want the herb to grow. Choose a light soil that has been nourished with manure or compost in advance, so that it will not dry out in the summer and encourage the plant to bolt. Coriander/cilantro prefers light shade to full sun as young plants are prone to scorching. You can also sow the seeds into a large, deep pot if you are growing in containers. In a small pot of soil there will be little space for the tap root and the herb will produce few leaves before it flowers and goes to seed.

VIETNAMESE PHO

I tried this soup for the first time when it was offered for breakfast during a holiday in Vietnam. Cafés by the roadside were full of people enjoying pho to kick-start their day. But by adding enough chicken, beansprouts and noodles, I now have it regularly for lunch at home. Its spicy freshness depends a lot on the wonders of coriander/cilantro. I often make double the quantity of flavoured stock and freeze half to use as the base for pho on another day.

1 large onion, quartered
6cm/2½in piece of root ginger
1 litre/35fl oz/4⅓ cups chicken stock
3 star anise
2 tsp coriander seeds
1 tsp fennel seeds
3 cardamom pods
2 tbsp caster/superfine sugar
3 tbsp nam pla (Thai fish sauce)
1 red chilli, deseeded and sliced
2 skinless, boneless chicken breasts, sliced
300g/10½oz packet of straight-to-wok rice noodles
2 handfuls of beansprouts
juice of 1 lime, to taste
4 small handfuls coriander/cilantro leaves

Grill/broil the onion and ginger for about 10 minutes until they start to blacken.

Heat the stock to boiling and add the onion, ginger, spices, sugar, fish sauce and chilli and simmer for 15 minutes. This can be done in advance and left for the flavours to develop. Strain to remove the herbs, vegetables and spices, then pour the chicken stock back into a saucepan and bring to the boil. Add the sliced chicken and simmer for several minutes until it is cooked. Then add the noodles and cook for 2 minutes. Add lime juice to taste. Check the flavours to make sure the balance with fish sauce and sugar is correct and adjust as necessary.

Ladle into bowls and add the beansprouts and coriander/cilantro just before serving.

Serves 4

Preparation: 18 mins
Cooking: 35 mins

1 fillet of beef, about 1kg/
  2lb 4oz, rolled and tied
sea salt and freshly ground
  black pepper
1 lime, quartered, to serve

SOY MARINADE
2 tbsp soy sauce
1 tbsp sesame oil
2 tbsp vegetable oil

HERB SALAD
2 tbsp lime juice
2 tbsp soy sauce
1 tbsp sesame oil
1 tsp sugar
1 small red chilli, deseeded and
  chopped
4 small red onions, finely sliced
4 spring onions/scallions, sliced
2 handfuls of coriander/cilantro,
  leaves picked and roughly
  chopped
1 handful of mint, leaves picked
  and roughly chopped
1 handful of basil, leaves picked
  and roughly chopped
1 handful of flatleaf parsley,
  leaves picked and roughly
  chopped

NEW POTATOES
16 small new potatoes
3 tbsp olive oil
1 tbsp chopped rosemary or
  thyme leaves

Preparation: 30 mins
Cooking: 45 mins

CORIANDER CELEBRATION FILLET OF BEEF

This is an expensive but very special dish, which looks beautiful with the beef sliced and arranged with the salad and potatoes on a large white platter. It brings a modern twist to the old standby of rare, sliced beef, with the sweet, hot, lime and herby tang of a quality Thai salad. This is perfect to serve out in the garden on a hot summer day. It is definitely a family favourite.

Mix together the marinade ingredients, pour over the beef, cover and leave in a cool place overnight.

Preheat the oven to 190°C/375°F/Gas 5. Toss the potatoes in the oil and herb and season with salt and pepper. Roast for about 45 minutes until tender and crisp on the outside. After 10 minutes, put the beef in the oven and cook for 30 minutes maximum until it is still pink in the middle. Leave it to rest while the potatoes finish cooking.

Just before serving, mix together all the salad ingredients. Slice the beef and put on a large serving plate, arrange the potatoes around the edge and sprinkle the salad over the top. Garnish the plate with lime quarters and serve the remaining salad on the side.

Serves 8–12

OKRA WITH CORIANDER AND TOMATO

When I moved from North-East England to West London, one of the many great culinary thrills was the closeness of Southall, with its shops, cafés and restaurants serving the local Indian community. I had never seen many of the Asian vegetables and herbs before, or the sweet, sugary cakes and bottles of pickles. I always went home with different things to try and never missed buying unusual vegetables and huge bunches of coriander/cilantro and flatleaf parsley. Okra soon became a regular dish, cooked in a variety of ways. This is still a favourite.

2 tbsp olive oil
2 large onions, chopped
6 garlic cloves, finely chopped
900g/2lb fresh young okra,
  trimmed and chopped into
  1cm/½in lengths
1kg/2lb 4oz tomatoes, skinned,
  deseeded and chopped
  (see page 24), about
  400g/14oz prepared weight
2 tbsp lemon juice
2 tsp ground coriander
1 handful of coriander/cilantro,
  leaves picked and chopped
sea salt and freshly ground
  black pepper

Heat the oil in a large frying pan and soften the onions for about 10 minutes over a gentle heat. Add the garlic and fry for a couple of minutes, then add the okra and cook for 2 minutes. Add the tomatoes, lemon juice and ground coriander, then season with salt and pepper and bring to the boil. Turn down the heat to low and gradually add 180ml/6fl oz/¾ cup water, keeping the sauce simmering for about 15 minutes until the okra is tender and the sauce is thick. Serve sprinkled with the fresh coriander/cilantro.

Serves 4

Preparation: 20 mins
Cooking: 30 mins

QUINOA AND CORIANDER SALAD

This is a healthy and tasty salad, which can be made with vegetables, nuts or fruit. In the summer months you can ring the changes by combining chopped fresh peaches or nectarines with pistachios, raisins, spring onions/scallions and rocket/arugula, but this salad works beautifully with these vegetables, too.

200g/7oz/scant 1¼ cups quinoa
½ small cauliflower, cut into small florets
1 large bunch of coriander/cilantro, leaves picked
4 tbsp olive oil
12 small mushroom caps
3 spring onions/scallions, chopped
2–3 sundried tomatoes in oil, drained and quartered
juice of 2 lemons
sea salt and freshly ground black pepper

Preheat the oven to 180°C/350°F/Gas 4. Put the quinoa in a saucepan, just cover with water and add a pinch of salt. Bring to the boil, then simmer for 12 minutes until the quinoa is tender. Drain, then spread the quinoa out on a plate and leave it to cool and dry.

Meanwhile, cook the cauliflower in boiling water for 3 minutes until cooked but still slightly crunchy. Drain and put in a roasting pan.

Put a quarter of the coriander/cilantro leaves in a small blender with the oil and blend until smooth. Pour the herby oil over the mushrooms, then season with salt and pepper. Put in the roasting pan with the cauliflower, then cook them in the oven for 10 minutes until cooked but still crisp.

Chop the remaining coriander/cilantro leaves, then stir them into the quinoa. Add the mushrooms, cauliflower, spring onions/scallions and sundried tomatoes, then sprinkle over the lemon juice to serve.

Serves 4

Preparation: 20 mins
Cooking: 25 mins

CORIANDER

ROSEMARY

Rosemary was originally a Mediterranean herb, but is now found in most parts of the world and is used in recipes by everyone with the slightest interest in food. It is so adaptable that it can be grown in a pot inside or out, it can be cut into elegant shapes or used as a small hedge to protect other less hardy herbs. I find I use it at least once a week in my recipes, so make sure you have it growing not too far away from your kitchen.

HISTORY

According to legend, rosemary was draped around the Greek goddess Aphrodite as she rose from the sea. In the past, it was thought that disease came from dirty air, so rosemary was used a lot during the Plague when people carried posies of herbs and scented flowers to ward off disease. It featured in funerals too, thrown over the coffin as it was lowered into the earth.

Lots of myths surround this herb, one being that it will grow for 33 years before it dies because the length of Christ's life was 33 years. The Virgin Mary is also said to have laid her blue cloak over a rosemary bush with white flowers when she stopped for a rest. The flowers were thought to have become blue at that moment, so the herb then became known as the Rose of Mary.

COOKING

I use the youngest leaves from the tips for cooking and I also use straight stems with their leaves cut back a little as aromatic kebab sticks to push through chunks of vegetables, chicken or lamb. Add rosemary to bouquet garni, to stuffings, for spiking meat and game, in herb oils, vinegars and marinades and with new potatoes, onions or vegetables, roasted in olive oil.

Rosemary is certainly one of the most special and versatile of culinary herbs. It is powerful for flavouring all meat, especially lamb, as well as fish, tomato dishes, beans and lemon sauces. Rosemary Syrup (see page 213) is a favourite in many of my desserts. I also make Apple Jelly flavoured with rosemary (see page 166), which is useful in fruit tart recipes (see page 129). I always make lots of apple and rosemary jelly because when I have plenty of fruit, from white currants to apples and pears, I make individual tarts or a large tart with puff pastry, covered with fruit slices. I then add finely chopped fresh rosemary and finish with a thick layer of the jelly, which sweetens and glazes the tart instantly.

GROWING

Most species have blue flowers, although I have grown white or pink plants, which seem less hardy. The bushy Corsican rosemary is good for cooking, and I like the prostrate rosemary grown over walls and in urns, but my favourite for its looks and taste is Miss Jessopp's Upright. In flavour tests of over 30 types of rosemary by a food company, this variety came top.

Rosemary can look very beautiful, is trouble free and, once planted, ideally in spring in well-drained soil, will often last for decades. It demands little attention, needing a prune only once a year. I cut my plants back after the winter flowers are over, but rosemary can also be pruned in the autumn. I grow it as a fan shape against south-facing walls and as a standard. It is also perfect for topiary fans, but to be successful, start to shape the plant when young. If you want to train this type of rosemary as a hedge, start with small plants 46cm/18in apart.

The best way to grow the less hardy varieties of rosemary, especially in cold areas, is in pots. You may need to protect them with fleece in freezing conditions. Always use well-drained soil wherever you are planting rosemary, incorporating some grit with the compost. Do not overwater and feed only after flowering.

Rosemary is easy to propagate from softwood cuttings. In late spring, take 8cm/3in cuttings from young shoots and treat in the normal way. The great thing about rosemary is that it grows easily in the garden to use fresh for 12 months a year. Some people hang bunches to dry in the kitchen, but I find that the leaves fall to the ground like Christmas tree needles and taste disgusting.

ROSEMARY AND COURGETTE QUICHE

It is worth using both green and yellow courgettes/zucchini for the quiche because it will look more attractive. Rosemary is the perfect herb to cook with this vegetable, for the following recipe and many others.

PASTRY

225g/8oz/1¾ cups plain/all-purpose white flour or sieved wholemeal/whole-wheat flour, plus extra for dusting

a pinch of salt

110g/4oz/scant ½ cup butter, plus extra for greasing

1 egg, beaten with 1½ tbsp water

FILLING

30g/1oz/2 tbsp butter

1 onion, finely chopped

1 garlic clove, chopped

175g/6oz green courgettes/zucchini, sliced

175g/6oz yellow courgettes/zucchini, sliced

2 eggs

120ml/4fl oz/½ cup double/heavy cream

4 tbsp grated Parmesan cheese

1 tbsp finely chopped young rosemary leaves

sea salt and freshly ground black pepper

mixed green salad including courgette/zucchini, to serve

Preparation: 45 mins, plus chilling
Cooking: 1 hr

To make the pastry, sift the flour and salt onto a kitchen work surface. Make a well in the middle and put the butter and egg into the well. Work them together using your fingertips until they are mixed, then gradually draw in the flour. Toss it until it has a sandy texture. Gather into a ball, work with the heel of the hand, gather up again, work and repeat a third time. Put in a plastic bag or wrap in cling film/plastic wrap and chill in the refrigerator for 1 hour.

Preheat the oven to 180°C/350°F/Gas 4 and grease a 23cm/9in flan dish. Roll out the pastry on a lightly floured surface and use to line the flan dish. Put a piece of baking parchment over the pastry and cover with baking beans. Bake for 10 minutes, then remove the paper and beans.

To make the filling, melt the butter in a frying pan over a medium heat and soften the onion for 10 minutes, then add the garlic and fry for a further 2 minutes. Add the courgettes/zucchini and fry for 3 minutes.

Beat the eggs in a bowl with the cream, add the cheese, season with salt and pepper, then mix with the cooked vegetables and chopped rosemary. Pour into the pastry case and bake for about 30 minutes until golden brown. Serve with a green salad including finely sliced raw courgette/zucchini.

Serves 4

DUCK WITH SEVILLE ORANGE AND ROSEMARY SAUCE

I first tried this recipe in Elizabeth David's *French Provincial Cookery* when I was learning to cook. I have modified it over the years, serving it with farmed or wild duck. The distinctive Bigarade sauce, named after the French name for Seville oranges, can only be made when they are in the shops, but I like it so much that I freeze small pots to use throughout the year. The house smells of sharp Seville oranges for days because I buy enough oranges to make plenty of my mother's "magic marmalade" too, which includes extra lemons to provide a fresh, sharp taste that I have never found in a professional jar. Marmalade-making sums up an agreement between my mother and me. When I was busy with children and work at the BBC, she made enough marmalade to keep the Hann toast tasty; it was typical of the support she always gave me. When she became frail, our roles reversed. She never had to buy marmalade, nor, I hope, worry about a thing.

4 duck breasts
1 tbsp butter
1 tbsp plain/all-purpose flour
1 tbsp chopped young rosemary leaves
90ml/3fl oz/6 tbsp dry white wine
90ml/3fl oz/6 tbsp stock, made from duck giblets if you have them, or chicken stock
finely grated zest and juice of 3 Seville oranges
about 1–3 tbsp redcurrant jelly, to taste
sea salt and freshly ground black pepper

Preparation: 30 mins
Cooking: 45 mins

To cook the duck, score the fatty skin on the breasts. Heat a heavy-based frying pan, put the duck breasts skin-side down in the pan and dry-fry for 12–15 minutes until the skin is golden brown. Pour off the fat. Add salt and pepper to the breasts, turn them over in the pan and cook for several minutes until they are cooked to your liking.

Meanwhile, make the sauce. Heat the butter in a saucepan over a medium heat until it starts to brown, then add the flour and cook, stirring continuously, until you have a pale brown roux. Add the rosemary and the wine and heat until reduced a little. Add the stock and simmer until you have a smooth, thick sauce the consistency of double/heavy cream. Add the orange zest to the sauce with the juice from the oranges and simmer for a few minutes. When you taste it you will find it bitter, but you can then add enough redcurrant jelly to suit your taste buds. Start with 1 tablespoon, but you will probably want to add more. Season with salt and pepper. Slice the duck breasts and serve with the sauce.

Serves 4

LAMB KEBABS WITH ROSEMARY VEGETABLES

Shish kebab must be the most famous Turkish dish. It is thought to have been first created in the Ottoman Empire when Turkish soldiers, forced to camp in tents, grilled/broiled their food over wood outside. I like to use rosemary stems for vegetable kebabs. They add so much flavour. You should marinate the vegetable and lamb kebabs first and, if possible, grill/broil them over dried herbs to improve the taste even more. A local blacksmith made me a large metal spit to use over the open fire in my kitchen. Dried rosemary, thyme, sage, bay and even lavender are always on hand when I am using the spit. Pheasant, partridge, and smaller dishes like kebabs, are cooked over our own dried wood, often collected after pruning apple and pear trees.

1 large neck fillet of lamb, about 500g/1lb 2oz, cut into small squares
16 small tomatoes
16 small mushroom caps
2 yellow peppers, deseeded and cut into 16 pieces
4 straight rosemary stems to use for the vegetables kebabs
2 tbsp sumac (optional)

HERB MARINADE
90ml/3fl oz/6 tbsp olive oil
2 tbsp chopped rosemary leaves
4 bay leaves
sea salt and freshly ground black pepper
juice of 2 lemons

TO SERVE
4 pitta breads
Tabbouleh (see page 60) or rice
dressed salad herb leaves

Mix together all the marinade ingredients, pour half over the lamb, cover and leave to marinate at room temperature for at least 2 hours, turning occasionally. Marinate the tomatoes, mushroom caps and peppers in the remaining marinade for 1 hour.

Drain the meat and thread onto 4 metal or soaked wooden skewers. Sprinkle with the sumac, if using. Thread the tomatoes, mushrooms and peppers onto 4 rosemary stems, one for each person. Grill/broil both the lamb and the vegetable kebabs on a fire, a barbecue or under a very hot grill/broiler for no more than 10 minutes, turning occasionally, when the vegetables will be cooked and the outside of the meat should be brown, but the inside pink and juicy.

Warm the pitta bread for 1 minute under the grill/broiler. Serve the kebabs and pitta with Tabbouleh or rice and a herb salad.

Serves 4

Preparation: 30 mins, plus marinating
Cooking: 12 mins

ICED PEAR SOUFFLÉ

This is the most poetic pudding I serve, special enough for any occasion. It looks so elegant made in small, individual circular moulds with a poached pear sitting in the middle of each one, decorated with fresh rosemary. Poach the pears in sugar, white wine and a rosemary sprig, based on the recipe on page 176. This soufflé can be made with other fruit purées, but made with pears it is white, light and bright. I sometimes make huge bowls of it, as well as pouring the mixture into small dishes. If you are making ice cream or crème brûlée, you can use the egg whites left over from those recipes to make this delicious concoction.

400g/14oz pears, peeled, cored and cut into chunks
juice of 1 lemon
2 sprigs of rosemary
280g/10oz/scant 1½ cups caster/superfine sugar
5 egg whites
300ml/10½fl oz/1¼ cups double/heavy cream, whipped
4 tbsp pear liqueur or 1 recipe quantity Rosemary Syrup (see page 213)

Start by making the pear purée. Put the pear flesh, lemon juice and rosemary in a saucepan and simmer until the pears are tender – about 10 minutes. Discard the rosemary and purée the fruit and juice in a food processor.

To make the Italian meringue, dissolve the sugar in 120ml/4fl oz/½ cup water over a low heat, then raise the heat, bring to the boil and boil hard until you reach the hard ball stage (120°C/248°F). If you don't have a sugar thermometer, take out a little of the syrup on a teaspoon and dip it into iced water, then knead it between your fingers – if it forms a firm, pliable ball, it is ready.

Whisk the egg whites until soft peaks form, then pour the sugar syrup over them, whisking all the time until the meringue swells. Fold the whipped cream and pear liqueur, if using, into the meringue, then fold in the cooled fruit purée. Pour the mixture into a large dish, or individual pots, and place in the freezer. You can store it in the freezer for up to 3 months.

Before you are ready to serve, remove the soufflé from the freezer and allow it to soften a little. You want it to be halfway between a cold soufflé and ice cream. If you are not using liqueur in the recipe, you can serve the soufflé with rosemary syrup poured over the top.

Preparation: 45 mins, plus freezing
Cooking: 15 mins

Serves 4–6

APPLE AND ROSEMARY CAKE

I like the flavour of rosemary with apple dishes, and rosemary syrup adds an important oomph to this cake, which can be eaten at teatime or served as a dessert with cream or ice cream. If you are using this as a dessert, you may want to double the quantity of rosemary syrup so that you can pour a little more onto each individual slice of cake, adding some extra vanilla sugar and lemon zest.

650g/1lb 7oz eating/dessert apples, peeled, cored and sliced

finely grated zest and juice of 1 lemon

4 eggs

140g/5oz/scant ¾ cup caster/ superfine sugar

140g/5oz/heaped 1 cup plain/ all-purpose flour

1 tsp baking powder

a pinch of salt

115g/4oz/½ cup unsalted butter, melted

1 tbsp very finely chopped rosemary leaves

vanilla sugar, for sprinkling

ROSEMARY SYRUP

15g/½oz rosemary sprigs

2 tbsp caster/superfine sugar

Preparation: 35 mins
Cooking: 40 mins

Preheat the oven to 180°C/350°F/Gas 5. Grease a 23cm/9in cake pan and line the base with parchment paper. Mix the apples with the lemon juice.

Put the eggs and sugar in a bowl and whisk well until pale and fluffy. Sift half the flour, all the baking powder and the salt over the mixture and fold in. Gently add the melted butter, the rest of the flour, the chopped rosemary and then the apple slices. Mix well. Spoon into the prepared pan and bake for 40 minutes until a skewer inserted in the middle comes out clean.

Meanwhile, make the rosemary syrup. Wash the rosemary and put the small sprigs into a pan with the sugar and 5 tablespoons of water. Cook over a low heat for about 10 minutes until the sugar has turned into a clear syrup and the rosemary has crystallized.

Remove the cake from the oven and leave to cool in the pan for about 5 minutes, then turn it out of the pan onto a serving plate. Pour the rosemary syrup over the top and it will soon soak through the cake, adding its wonderful flavour. Keep the cake at room temperature, covered, and it will last for days. Sprinkle with vanilla sugar and the lemon zest before serving.

Makes a 23cm/9in cake

SALAD HERBS AND ROCKET

Salad herbs are now the stars on our plates, despite the fact that they were rarely seen, sold, grown or eaten a few decades ago. Today there are dozens of different plants of many colours, shapes and textures, like the ever-popular rocket/arugula, many types of cress, Japanese species like mizuna and shungiku and mustards of every size and taste. I like to mix them on a plate as a base for favourite recipes.

HISTORY

Our most popular salad herb, rocket/arugula, was virtually unknown for centuries, despite being part of culinary life for the Romans and then the French and Italians. So it surprises many people to know that it was listed by John Evelyn in the 17th century as being an important British salad herb. He described it as: "Hot and dry, to be qualified with lettuce", realizing it is wise to mix it with less punchy salad ingredients. John Evelyn's definition of a salad is: "In a sallet every plant should come in to bear its part without being over-powered by some herb of a stronger taste, but fall into their places like the notes in music".

My inspiration was the writer and gardener, Joy Larkam, who travelled the world from the 1970s, bringing back seeds to try at home. Her books, *The Salad Garden* and *Oriental Vegetables*, taught me so much, too, explaining the pleasure of oriental varieties and Japanese salad leaves. She even learned Chinese to make her research more successful and her descriptions remind me of a filming trip I made for the BBC to Yunnan Province in South China, where vegetables and salad herbs are grown everywhere in perfectly tended fields. It inspired me to grow as many varieties as possible in my own garden at home.

COOKING

Most of my salad herbs are served raw, but almost all of them can also be cooked for soups, stir-fries and sauces. Younger leaves of salad herbs have a milder, fresher taste than older ones, so they are perfect for salads, such as my Middle Eastern-inspired Winter Salad of Mixed Herbs, Squash and Pomegranate (see page 222). They get more peppery as they get older and these leaves are more suitable for wilting into crushed new potatoes or folding into a tomato sauce to be served with pasta.

Rocket/arugula leaves are perfect for sprinkling onto pizzas or into soup. Or blend them into a pesto with a real oomph (see page 35). Pesto is useful to serve with pasta, as a topping for tarts, in different canapés and for tossing with new potatoes. It will keep in the refrigerator for a week and can also be frozen. In the Gulf of Naples, rocket/arugula is also used to make a powerful liqueur.

VARIETIES I GROW

My salad herb bed is a work of art with broad-leaf sorrel edging the beds and alpine strawberries at the front. Red-veined sorrel grows in a circle in the middle with other salad herbs sown likes spokes of a wheel, using contrasting colours and leaf shapes. I use dramatic leaves like mizuna as the spokes and in between I sow smaller salad leaves like purslane and lamb's lettuce/corn salad.

JAPANESE SALAD HERBS

MITSUBA or Japanese parsley. This is a small clumping perennial which tastes rather like nutty, celery flavoured parsley. It likes shade and is used traditionally in salads, miso soup and sushi.

MIZUNA is popular in the West with its dark green, divided leaves and fresh, peppery taste. Use it like rocket/arugula.

MIBUNA has a long history of cultivation in Mibu, which is in the Kyoto area. Its long narrow leaves have a stronger flavour than mizuna.

SHUNGIKU or chop suey greens. This is an attractive, edible chrysanthemum with petals and leaves used for their gentle aniseed flavour in salads or stir-fries. In Japan it is one of the most popular leafy herbs, found in markets everywhere. I only use the leaves and flower petals, because the middle of the flower is very bitter.

MUSTARD GREENS

Red Frills is my favourite mustard because its delicate, maroon frilly leaves look so good on the plate. I also grow Golden Streaks mustard, with similar-shaped leaves of a golden colour. Slugs leave mustards alone because they do not fancy their peppery leaves. In past years I have grown the bigger leaves of Red Giant and Green in the Snow mustards.

WINTER PURSLANE, or claytonia, is one of the hardiest salad herbs, with pretty heart-shaped fleshy leaves and edible white flowers. It has a mild taste with a hint of violets. It is high in vitamin C and works well mixed with spicy leaves like rocket/arugula.

SUMMER PURSLANE with golden leaves is also worth growing. It has succulent round leaves and crunchy, edible buds, which taste of mangetout/snow peas.

LAMB'S LETTUCE, also known as corn salad, has attractive rosettes of mild, nutty, oval green leaves, which look good on the plate and bulk out more flavoursome leaves.

GREEK CRESS is a peppery plant with attractive divided leaves. I use it as much as rocket/arugula for its superb taste and looks and also grow other types of cress like Bubbles and Wrinkled Crinkled. Cress is often given silly names.

LAND CRESS grows well in winter and in shade and has a useful watercress taste for salads, soups and sauces. Pick the leaves young for salads, when they are 8–10cm/3–4in high. It looks good for edging salad herb beds.

PERILLA, also known as shiso, has green or red varieties, with a taste of cumin, aniseed or cinnamon. Young leaves have the best flavour for salads. Plant 30cm/12in apart in rich, well-drained soil in a sunny spot. Once the plants are established, pinching out the growing tips encourages bushy, leafy growth.

RED ORACH is a hardy annual, cultivated in Asia and south-eastern Europe for centuries. Its maroon leaves have an intense flavour and, when small, can be used in salads, or cooked like spinach when they are more mature. It grows to 1m/39in, with large attractive seed heads.

MIXED LEAVES

When you want to grow a variety of salad herbs in a small space, like a window box, use a packet of mixed salad herbs, called Oriental Saladini or Mesclun, and sow the seeds more densely than normal. The first cut can often be made within three to four weeks, when the seedlings are 6cm/2½in high. Cut again whenever they reach that height.

MICRO HERBS are fashionable to decorate a plate and bring intense flavour. You can experiment at home using a seed tray on a windowsill. Pick when they are about 2.5cm/1in tall and have their first set of true leaves.

DANDELION first came into my culinary life on my 40th birthday. I was celebrating in Monte Carlo's Hermitage Hotel, eating a salad of dandelion leaves, mushrooms and bacon in a beautiful dressing. Wanting to recreate this at home, I bought a packet of *pissenlit* seeds the next day. Back at home, where I shared an allotment with my father, he refused to consider growing dandelions there. "I have spent hours digging the damn things up. Throw the seeds away", he said. But I have been growing them in my own herb garden for 20 years. The cultivated leaves are superior to wild dandelion, with larger, milder leaves.

ROCKET

Rocket/arugula is the most useful salad herb I grow. I always have some in the herb garden because it survives the winter conditions well.

There are two types of rocket/arugula: salad and wild. Salad rocket/arugula is an annual with cream flowers, which are also edible. There are many varieties, including a red-veined variety called Dragon's Tongue and one launched in 2016 that tastes of the Japanese mustard, wasabi. In general, the narrower and more indented the leaf, the more peppery the flavour of the variety will be. The second type is the much stronger-tasting perennial wild plant. It is useful to have this as a permanent crop.

GROWING

Twice a year, in mid-spring and late summer, you should be sowing salad herbs to provide an all-year supply. Whether you are growing them in a container or in the garden, mix the varieties to get an attractive combination of colours, shapes and textures.

You can grow salad herbs as "cut-and-come again", harvesting regularly. This is a great advantage, because buying bags of salads can be expensive and the leaves are never as fresh as those in your garden or window box. Bought salad leaves are also stripped of vitamins by the "modified atmosphere" process often used to lengthen their shelf lives.

People are surprised to find that salad herbs, sown in late summer, will grow throughout the winter. But, in fact, they thrive in the colder months. Unlike herbs sown in spring, they do not bolt or become full of holes from the flea beetle. They often have a better size and flavour. When they become very mature in late winter, I leave them for a couple of hours in water to rehydrate. This gives them an improved texture.

When I am about to sow seeds, I water the soil thoroughly to avoid splashing the small seeds around once sown. After sowing, I cover the seed with fine compost, add some organic fertilizer if the soil needs help and keep the area moist but not overwatered. Once the plants have matured, I harvest them regularly to prevent them going to seed. I twist or pinch off lower leaves, leaving a rosette of three or four small leaves in the middle. These quickly grow for the next harvest and plants can be cropped for up to three months using this technique. Pick leaves off some plants to eat, but also eat some small whole plants to make space for other plants to mature.

TOMATO AND ROCKET TART

This is the easiest tart to make and it has great flavour. Instead of using cream cheese on the pastry base, a soft goats' cheese is good, too. I sometimes also add other vegetables to the tomato, like aubergine/eggplant, peppers or courgette/zucchini, sliced and browned in a little olive oil. Other herbs can be used to make the pesto topping if you prefer. It can be served hot or cold, as one large tart or made into individual smaller tarts.

a little olive oil, for greasing
375g/13oz pack of ready-rolled
    puff pastry
200g/7oz/scant 1 cup soft
    cream cheese
450g/1lb tomatoes, sliced
1 recipe quantity Classic Pesto
    made with rocket/arugula
    (see page 35)
sea salt and freshly ground
    black pepper
mixed green salad, including
    rocket/arugula, to serve

Preheat the oven to 180°C/350°F/Gas 4 and lightly oil a 30 x 40cm/ 12 x 16in baking sheet.

Place the pastry on the baking sheet and use a knife to score a line round the pastry about 1cm/½in from the edge without cutting the pastry all the way through to the baking sheet. Spread the cheese over the surface, making sure that you get it right up to the line you have just cut in the pastry.

Arrange the sliced tomatoes on top of the cheese, then season with salt and pepper. Bake in the oven for 20–30 minutes until the pastry is golden and the tomatoes cooked. Spread the pesto over the tart while it is still very hot, so that it starts to melt into the tomatoes. Serve with a mixed green salad, including rocket/arugula leaves, of course.

Serves 4

Preparation: 20 mins
Cooking: 30 mins

HERBY GRILLED CHICKEN WITH ROCKET, SUNDRIED TOMATO AND OLIVE SALAD

90ml/3fl oz/6 tbsp olive oil
1 tbsp chopped rosemary leaves
2 garlic cloves, finely chopped
grated zest and juice of 1 lemon
4 skinless chicken breasts
sea salt and freshly ground
  black pepper

MUSTARD DRESSING
2 tbsp Dijon mustard
2 tbsp white wine vinegar
120ml/4fl oz/½ cup sunflower
  or groundnut oil

ROCKET, SUNDRIED TOMATO
  AND OLIVE SALAD
140g/5oz rocket/arugula leaves
1 small handful of basil leaves,
  purple if available
16 black olives, pitted
10 sundried tomatoes in oil,
  chopped
55g/2oz Parmesan cheese,
  shaved

Warm salads can be marvellous – or they can turn into a disaster if you cannot persuade your diners to sit down at the table on time! I find they are usually chatting so much that they dawdle, so have learned to get them sitting down before I assemble the warm ingredients with the rocket/arugula or salad herbs.

Mix together the oil, rosemary, garlic and lemon zest and juice, seasoning with salt and pepper. Pour over the chicken, cover and leave in the refrigerator for at least 3 hours.

Preheat the grill/broiler to high. Lift the chicken out of the marinade and season with salt and pepper. Grill/broil for about 8 minutes on each side until cooked through and nicely browned.

Meanwhile, make the mustard dressing. Put the mustard, vinegar and 4 tablespoons of warm water in a blender and mix well. With the motor running, gradually add the oil until it thickens to a thin mayonnaise. Season to taste with salt and pepper.

Mix together the rocket/arugula, basil, olives and sundried tomatoes and toss in a little of the dressing. Arrange on the sides of four plates and top with the Parmesan shavings. Slice the chicken on the diagonal and arrange on the plates to serve, with the remaining dressing on the side.

Serves 4

Preparation: 20 mins, plus marinating
Cooking: 16 mins

SALAD HERBS WITH SMOKED DUCK AND SPICED PEARS

It is important for the look of this dish that some red or maroon leaves, like perilla or mustards, are used with the green leaves to pick up the colour of the smoked duck. The last time I served this, I added buckler-leaf sorrel leaves, winter purslane and a little chervil, too. The spiced pears look elegant at the middle of a plate of leaves with thin slices of duck. I am lucky to have a high-quality smokery nearby, where it is possible to buy a huge variety of smoked meats, fish, cheese and even strings of smoked garlic, but these days you can buy smoked duck in the supermarket, too.

4 Spiced Pears with Herbs (see page 167)
400g/14oz mixed salad herb leaves and other
  small herbs
4 tbsp Mustard Dressing (see page 221)
3 smoked duck breasts, thinly sliced

This is as simple as placing a spiced pear in the middle of each plate. Toss the salad leaves in the dressing, then arrange around the edge with the slices of smoked duck like spokes of a wheel around the pear.

Serves 4

Preparation: 15 mins

POACHED FIGS, FETA AND SALAD HERBS

This dish makes use of dried figs when fresh ones are hard to find or are rather tasteless in mid-winter – a time when salad herbs are often at their very best.

12 dried figs
500ml/17fl oz/generous 2 cups grape juice
400g/14oz mixed baby salad herbs
175g/6oz feta cheese, crumbled
40g/1½oz/heaped ¼ cup pine nuts, toasted
2 tbsp olive oil
sea salt and freshly ground black pepper

Put the dried figs and grape juice in a saucepan, bring to the boil, then simmer gently for 15 minutes until soft. Leave to cool, then lift out of the poaching liquid using a slotted spoon and cut into quarters.

Arrange the salad herbs on four plates, top with the figs and scatter the feta and pine nuts on the leaves.

Mix the oil with 2 tablespoons of the poaching liquid and spoon over the salad. Season with salt and pepper and serve.

Serves 4

Preparation: 20 mins
Cooking: 20 mins

WINTER SALAD OF MIXED HERBS, SQUASH AND POMEGRANATE

This is good to serve in autumn or winter when squash is at its best and the warm colours of the squash, the pomegranate and the mixed salad herbs make it look very enticing.

450g/1lb butternut or similar squash, peeled, deseeded and cut into small cubes
1 tbsp olive oil, plus extra for greasing
60g/2oz/scant ½ cup pine nuts
2 handfuls of rocket/arugula or mixed salad herb leaves
4 tbsp pomegranate seeds
sea salt and freshly ground black pepper

POMEGRANATE DRESSING
200ml/7fl oz/scant 1 cup pomegranate molasses
60ml/2fl oz/¼ cup syrupy balsamic vinegar
1 tbsp olive oil
2 tsp Dijon mustard

Preheat the oven to 220°C/425°F/gas 7 and oil a roasting pan with a little olive oil. Put the cubes of squash in the pan, coat with the oil and season with salt and pepper. Roast for up to 40 minutes until soft inside and crisply browned on the edges, but test after 30 minutes to see if they are ready.

Meanwhile, in a small frying pan, fry the pine nuts for 2–3 minutes until lightly browned, then leave to cool. Whisk together all the dressing ingredients.

Divide the rocket/arugula onto four plates. Arrange the squash cubes on each plate, then top with the pine nuts and pomegranate seeds. Drizzle over the dressing and serve.

Serves 4

Preparation: 20 mins
Cooking: 40 mins

HERB CANAPÉS

Canapés are one part of the warm welcome I like to give to family and friends when they eat with us. Candles, the scent of flowers, a roaring fire and a beautifully set table. Everyone knows from the start that we are pleased to see them.

One of the most important things about canapés is that they should be simple enough to eat with poise. No host wants greasy olives falling off onto a cream sofa. No guest wants stains from unruly ingredients down their shirts and finely chopped herbs can be tiresome when they stick to your teeth. So bowl food, mini cones filled with squishy ingredients and canapés fitted into large china spoons are banned in this house. Canapés are often too ambitious and too large. Each one should be easy to consume in one or two mouthfuls.

I also make and freeze tiny pastry cases for canapés from leftover pastry. These can be filled with recipes like my Smoked Salmon and Herb Pâté or Chicken Liver Pâté with Apple and Herb (page 190), Tapenade (page 68), Classic Pesto (page 35), or the Mint and Pea Cream Cheese and Dill, Caper and Goats' Cheese recipes here. You can also buy small, thin pastry cups instead, or use small squares of rye bread.

When I have a large group of family or friends around to my house for a gathering, I often use a huge circular wooden board to serve the canapés. It is very old and despite having a handle many people have suggested it may have once been a cover from a well. Canapés of different shapes and colours look dramatic placed directly on the wood.

Each of these recipes makes about 20 canapés

DILL, CAPER AND GOATS' CHEESE CANAPÉ

This is a popular and refreshing canapé because of the combination of capers, lemon and dill. The speckled mixture, decorated with chopped dill, on rye squares looks inviting.

115g/4oz soft goats' cheese
2 tsp tiny capers, drained and rinsed
1 tsp lemon juice
a pinch of cayenne pepper
1 tbsp chopped dill, plus sprigs of dill to top
squares of rye bread or tiny pastry cases

Mix together the goats' cheese, capers, lemon juice, cayenne pepper and chopped dill. Spoon 1 teaspoon of the mixture onto squares of rye bread or into pastry cases and top with a sprig of dill.

[WHY NOT TRY...]

+ Rolling up small balls of soft goats' cheese and coating them in chopped herbs. Serve with a cocktail stick/ toothpick
+ Using the herb cheese from the Salami and Herb Cheese Rolls (see opposite) to fill small pastry tarts

ROSEMARY BUTTER NUTS

These rich and herby nuts make a real change from the normal cashew nuts, mixed nuts or gruesome peanuts that many people serve. The recipe will fill a decent-sized bowl for guests to dip in to.

250g/9oz unsalted nuts (cashews, hazelnuts, almonds, pine nuts, or a mixture)
40g/1½oz/3 tbsp butter
1 tbsp brown sugar
1 tsp sea salt
a pinch of cayenne pepper
needles from 1 sprig of rosemary, finely chopped

Preheat the oven to 170°C/325°F/Gas 3. Spread the nuts on a baking tray and bake for about 12 minutes – shaking and checking until they look golden. Then melt the butter, add the other ingredients and mix with the warm nuts. You can make them in advance.

MINI PIZZA SLICES

These tiny pizzas are simple to make and popular with everyone – even fussy, small children. No village event passes without me getting a request to make a large tray of these.

1 long, thin baguette, sliced into 24 x 1cm/½in thick slices
1 recipe quantity Tapenade (see page 68)
4 tomatoes, thinly sliced into 6 slices
400g/14oz mozzarella cheese, thinly sliced
12 pitted olives, halved or sliced

Preheat the oven to 200°C/400°F/Gas 6. Spread each slice of baguette with the tapenade. Top with a tomato slice, a thin slice of mozzarella and half a pitted olive. Place the pizza slices on a baking sheet and bake for about 10 minutes until the cheese is starting to brown.

MINT AND PEA CREAM CHEESE

This is a useful recipe, which not only can be used for canapés but can make individual-sized filo/phyllo parcels to serve with salad as a first course, or can be mixed into a basic egg quiche filling.

175g/6oz/1¼ cups fresh or frozen peas
140g/5oz/scant ⅔ cup cream cheese
2 tbsp chopped mint leaves, plus small leaves to top tiny pastry cases or squares of rye bread
sea salt and freshly ground black pepper

Cook the peas in boiling salted water for 3 minutes, or longer if frozen or the fresh peas are a little old when you buy or pick them. Drain them and leave to cool.

Put the peas in a food processor with the cream cheese, and chopped mint and season with salt and pepper. Blend everything together. Spoon about 1 teaspoon of the mixture into pastry cases or onto squares of rye bread and top with a small mint leaf.

SALAMI AND HERB CHEESE ROLLS

These rolls are delicious – small, tasty and herby. But the herb cheese alone, decorated with a sprig of the herb, is also a fine addition to a cheeseboard

250g/9oz/heaped 1 cup soft cream cheese
1 garlic clove, crushed
1 handful of lovage, chervil, dill or ½ handful of winter savory (as it has a strong flavour)
freshly ground black pepper
20 salami slices

Mix the cream cheese, garlic, herbs and seasoning well in a blender. Take a slice of salami, put 2 teaspoons of herbed cheese along the middle and roll up. Repeat with the other slices.

SWEET CICELY

Sweet cicely is a plant I enjoy for many reasons. It is one of the first herbs to poke through the soil in winter, offering its sweet-tasting leaves for favourite recipes. These delicate, fern-like leaves give a heady anise scent to food and they look beautiful in a vase, too, particularly when the creamy, white flowers appear. When visitors to my herb cookery courses taste dozens of different fresh herbs, they often choose sweet cicely as their favourite. This herb reduces the acidity of sharp ingredients like rhubarb, gooseberries and damsons, meaning you can use far less sugar in cooking.

HISTORY

Sweet cicely is native to the mountains of southern and central Europe from the Pyrenees to the Caucasus. The Greek called this herb *seseli* and its taste caused it to become known as sweet cicely. In the 16th century, the herb expert John Gerard boiled the roots of the herb and gave the sieved potion to patients who were feeling generally off-colour. The herbalist Nicholas Culpeper believed the roots protected people against the plague. Sweet cicely was also grown around graves, possibly because of its anise aroma. And it was rubbed into wood panelling to provide shine and sweet smells.

COOKING

The subtle aniseed taste of the leaves and seeds means sweet cicely has a lot in common with chervil. It is good with shellfish or incorporated into creamy sauces for fish or chicken. I also add finely chopped leaves to fruit salads, apple and pear flans, mixed green salads and cucumber dishes. The flavour can give an unusual lift to mayonnaise, omelettes and risotto. And drinks like wine cups also benefit from the anise taste with honey overtones. The roots are edible too and like caraway, anise and fennel, they are used to flavour the spirit *akvavit*. I often use the frothy flowers to decorate food. When the flowers and the fern-like leaves are at their best, sweet cicely is definitely the prettiest plant in my herb garden.

Sweet cicely makes it possible to use less sugar when you are cooking sharp fruit. All you have to do is add whole leaves and stalks to the fruit and then remove them after cooking. Long cooking does reduce the anise aroma, so it is often a good idea to stir in more leaves, finely chopped this time, into the cooked fruit just before serving. When the flowers turn to seed, the flavour of the leaves is reduced. So to avoid having to choose between useful seeds or flavoursome leaves, I always cut half of my sweet cicely plants to the ground when they are in flower, so that new tasty leaves have formed when the rest of the plants have seeds. The green seeds are full of aniseed flavour for adding chopped to puddings like Tarte Tatin with Sweet Cicely Seeds (see page 231), for shortbread biscuits, cream cheese, omelettes and salads. They are also wonderful for anise-flavoured ice cream.

GROWING

This herb is easy to grow in all conditions. It is a hardy perennial which grows to 1m/39in tall. The creamy flower umbels grow from spring into early summer, when they turn into green edible seeds. Sweet cicely is said to prefer shade and damp soil, but my plants also thrive in full sun and the dry corners of the pudding bed in the herb garden.

I never seem to manage to remove all the seeds before they fall onto the ground. After the early stages, when the seeds are green, soft and full of flavour, they become tough, black and inedible. Then they fall off the plant, eventually producing seedlings which are difficult to remove from areas where I do not want them. This is because it is hard to dig up the very long roots. If you leave even a small portion of root in the ground, a new plant will develop. They are not suitable for growing in pots because of this large tap root.

Sow the seeds outside in the autumn, where you want plants to grow. They need several months at low temperatures to germinate. Or you can sow them in a seed tray, cover with glass, and put them in a very cold corner outside. The other way to encourage germination is to put seeds into a small container of sand and keep in the refrigerator for a month. You can also propagate the plant by taking root cuttings in spring or autumn.

SWEET CICELY PLUM CRISP

Friday evenings were often a treat for me during my teenage years, when a close school friend invited me to join her family for the special meal to celebrate the Sabbath. Her grandfather was the leader of the very small Jewish community in Derby, UK and her mother was a great cook, inspired by her friend the famous cookery writer, Evelyn Rose. When I started to cook I bought *The Complete International Jewish Cookbook* by Evelyn and still use it occasionally. Her oat topping for a fruit crumble is very popular with my young granddaughters, who insist on making it themselves. When I cook this I double the quantity of oats and halve the quantity of sugar used from Evelyn's recipe. It is also excellent made with rhubarb, apples or pears.

500g/1lb 2oz plums, pitted
4 tbsp chopped sweet cicely
  leaves
a large pinch of ground
  cinnamon

MY OAT TOPPING
75g/3oz/scant ⅔ cup plain/
  all-purpose flour
50g/1¾oz/½ cup rolled oats
50g/1¾oz/scant ¼ cup light
  soft brown sugar
75g/2½oz/5 tbsp butter
cream, crème fraîche or vanilla
  ice cream, to serve

Preheat the oven to 190°C/375°F/Gas 5.

Rinse the plums and put them in a saucepan with a splash of water. Bring to the boil, then simmer gently for about 15 minutes until just soft; the time will depend on the size and ripeness of the plums.

Put the stewed plums into an attractive ovenproof dish large enough to hold the plums in one layer and deep enough to come about 5cm/2in above the plums. Scatter with the sweet cicely leaves and sprinkle with cinnamon. The herb adds sweetness to the plums so that no sugar is needed.

Combine the flour, oats and sugar, then rub in the butter until you have a crumbly mixture. Sprinkle in an even layer over the plums and bake for 30–40 minutes until the top is lightly browned and crunchy. Serve hot with cream, crème fraîche or vanilla ice cream.

Serves 4–6

Preparation: 25 mins
Cooking: 1 hr

TARTE TATIN WITH SWEET CICELY SEEDS

This is one of my favourite desserts, especially when we have lots of delicious, sharp apples. If the sweet cicely seeds are past their best, use finely chopped leaves instead. They have the same sweet aniseed taste. The seeds start off green, soft and very tasty, but darken and harden until they are not worth using. Serving apple sorbet or yogurt instead of cream or ice cream is a healthy option. And if you wanted to be experimental, you could try making your own ice cream (see pages 110–11), infusing the custard base with sweet cicely seeds or chopped leaves.

1.8kg/4lb sharp eating/dessert apples, like Granny Smiths
250g/9oz/1¼ cups caster/ superfine sugar
115g/4oz/½ cup unsalted butter
a large pinch of ground cinnamon
1 tbsp sweet cicely seeds, chopped
150g/5½oz sheet of puff pastry
cream or vanilla ice cream, to serve

Preheat the oven to 180°C/350°F/Gas 4. Peel and core the apples and cut into big pieces. Put 90g/3oz/scant ½ cup of the sugar in a 23cm/9in tarte tatin mould or ovenproof frying pan and heat gently for a few minutes over a low heat until it turns a dark caramel colour. Add half of the butter and let it melt, stirring, then remove from the heat. Pack the apple pieces tightly on top of the caramel. Dice the rest of the butter and dot it over the top, then sprinkle with the cinnamon, the chopped sweet cicely seeds and the remaining sugar. Bake in the oven for 25 minutes.

Cut a circle of pastry slightly larger than the mould and place it on the top of the fruit, tucking in the edges. Cook for a further 30 minutes until the pastry has started to brown. Leave to cool.

Put a flat plate on top of the tart, hold the plate and mould firmly and turn upside down so the tart drops out onto the plate. Serve with cream or vanilla ice cream.

Serves 4–6

Preparation: 30 mins
Cooking: 1 hr

SWEET CICELY

RHUBARB FOOL WITH SWEET CICELY

Sweet cicely dampens acidity when it is cooked with rhubarb, reducing the amount of sugar needed in the recipe. It also gives the dish an anise flavour. Fools are an old-fashioned food but people still love them and they are very easy to make. They are basically purées of sweetened fruit, with whipped cream swirled through. The finished fool should be the texture of softly whipped cream, so if it turns out too runny, add a little gelatine to the recipe. You can serve this dish immediately or chill it for several hours. Serve it with Thyme Shortbread (see page 129), with some chopped sweet cicely seeds added to the mix if available.

450g/1lb rhubarb
1 large sprig of sweet cicely
1 tbsp or more sugar, to taste
300ml/10½fl oz/1¼ cups
   double/heavy cream, whipped

Put the rhubarb and sweet cicely in a stainless steel pan with 2 tablespoons water and set over a low heat. Cook slowly at first, stirring, until the juices start to leave the rhubarb, then bring to the boil and simmer until soft. This will probably take about 10 minutes if it is young rhubarb, but it can take twice that time for older stems. Lift out the sweet cicely and stir the rhubarb with a wooden spoon. Taste for sweetness and you will find you will want to add some sugar. Do this gradually, 1 tablespoon at a time, to get it right. Leave to cool completely.

Fold the softly whipped cream into the cooled rhubarb, then spoon the fool into four dessert bowls or glasses to serve.

Serves 4

Preparation: 15 mins
Cooking: 20 mins

INDEX

ACKNOWLEDGMENTS

I would like to thank the Nourish team: particularly Rebecca Woods for her encouragement and impressive culinary knowledge, Tamin Jones for his beautiful photographs and Wendy Hobson, who found my book inspiring as she edited it into shape.

John, my husband, has always supported my passion for cooking with herbs and our older son Jake, who inherited my love and knowledge of food, has kept me on my toes with informed comments on new recipes.

His brother Daniel is the inspiration for my herb cookery school, Hann's Herbs. He had leukemia as a teenager and, after I planted my huge collection of herbs and used them constantly in the kitchen, he said that passing on my knowledge would be a perfect way of raising money for research into the disease. I am also grateful for help and guidance from Stella Mills in both the herb cookery school and garden.

ABOUT THE AUTHOR

Judith Hann is a broadcaster, journalist and author with a lifelong passion for herbs. She is a former President of the Herb Society and has written regularly for its magazine *Herbs*.

At her home in the Cotswolds, Judith runs a cookery school called Hann's Herbs and grows over 150 different culinary herbs in her garden, which has been filmed for Gardener's World and Rick Stein's *Food Heroes*. She also presented the BBC food series, *The Taste of Health*.

For 20 years Judith was the respected presenter of *Tomorrow's World* and wrote the best-selling book *How Science Works* (which sold over one million copies around the world).